Contract in Context

Contract in Context

**Richard Austen-Baker
and Qi Zhou**

Routledge
Taylor & Francis Group

LONDON AND NEW YORK

First published 2015
by Routledge
2 Park Square, Milton Park, Abingdon, Oxon OX14 4RN

and by Routledge
711 Third Avenue, New York, NY 10017

Routledge is an imprint of the Taylor & Francis Group, an informa business

© 2015 Richard Austen-Baker and Qi Zhou

The right of Richard Austen-Baker and Qi Zhou to be identified as authors of this work has been asserted by them in accordance with sections 77 and 78 of the Copyright, Designs and Patents Act 1988.

British Library Cataloguing in Publication Data
A catalogue record for this book is available from the British Library

Library of Congress Cataloging in Publication Data
    Austen-Baker, Richard, author.
    Contract in context / Richard Austen-Baker, Qi Zhou.
    pages cm
    1. Contracts. I. Zhou, Qi (Law teacher) author. II. Title.
    K840.A98 2014
    346.02'2—dc23
    2014008102

ISBN: 978-0-415-66316-8 (hbk)
ISBN: 978-0-415-66317-5 (pbk)
ISBN: 978-0-203-07165-6 (ebk)

Typeset in Baskerville
by Florence Production Ltd, Stoodleigh, Devon

Printed and bound in Great Britain by
TJ International Ltd, Padstow, Cornwall

Contents

Foreword

At a first glance, the choice of books that teachers of the law of contract may recommend their students to purchase is very large. Leaving aside the sort of book one sees, especially in the hands of students preparing for resit examinations, which is purchased even in the absence of any such recommendation, there are now in print more than a dozen creditable or highly creditable textbooks of various lengths and half a dozen casebooks of this quality. But in one area there is, I fear, an impending dearth.

By comparison to textbooks and casebooks, there has never been a large number of books that intend, not so much to give a textbook account of the law, but more directly to address, and to make accessible, the theoretical issues that a university education in contract worthy of the name should raise in students' minds. These are books that one can usefully ask students to read in preparation for their studies, and to which they can usefully turn for assistance in grasping essential themes throughout those studies. But despite their number being few, UK students have been particularly well provided with this sort of book. Leaving aside books out of print, Adams and Brownsword's *Understanding Contract Law*, first published in 1987 and now in its fifth edition of 2007, and Tillotson's *Contract Law in Perspective*, first published in 1981 and now in its fifth edition of 2008, having been given a new life by Mulcahy in a fourth edition of 2004, the fifth edition being her work alone, are, in their somewhat different ways, excellent.

But after the death in 2012 of John Adams, Professor Brownsword tells me he does not intend to bring out a new edition of *Understanding Contract Law*. And Professor Mulcahy, whose research was never mainly focused on contract and who has developed a range of quite different interests, tells me there will be no new edition of *Contract Law in Perspective*. One can, of course, ask the students to read the introductory chapters of a number of the better textbooks, but here again the future is unpromising, for the textbook that I personally would turn to first in this respect, Collins' *The Law of Contract*, now in its fourth edition of 2003, will also, I understand from Professor Collins, who has recently assumed the duties of the Vinerian Professor of English Law, not appear in a new edition.

The book for which I am very pleased to write this foreword will go some considerable way towards filling the gap left by these decisions. Its chapters set out in a coherent sequence most of the principal lines of theoretical inquiry to which the study of the law of contract should give rise. Chapter 1 discusses the function of contract, in the sense of an economic exchange, and the function of, quite a different thing, the law of contract. This discussion is based on Havighurst's 1961 Rosenthal Lectures on *The Nature of Private Contract*, so students will immediately benefit from being introduced to one of the outstanding contributions to contract theory. Chapter 2 is an overview of the history of the law of contract of similar scope to the one which the late Brian Simpson provided for *Cheshire, Fifoot and Furmston*, and which Professor Furmston now continues to provide with the distinguished assistance of Professor Ibbetson. Chapter 3 is a particularly valuable discussion of the concepts of classical and neo-classical contract, concepts to which students will see much reference made in the course of their studies, but of which a general statement readily comprehensible to them soon will be unavailable. Chapter 4 further develops the identification of the values of the classical law and begins a criticism of those values which wisely relies on *Understanding Contract Law*, which combined accessibility with depth of analysis in a remarkable way when explaining the tensions arising from the failures of the classical law in terms of dualisms of legal method and legal philosophy.

The heart of the book is, however, chapter 5, which gives a very clear account of the relational theory as an alternative to the classical and neo-classical law, and Chapters 6 and 7, which condense many of the best parts of the now immense, and immensely uneven, law and economics of contract. Although materials that would allow students to begin to examine the issues taken up in these chapters are gathered together particularly in Beale, Bishop and Furmston's *Contract, Cases and Materials*, now in a fifth edition of 2008, there really is nothing for students like these chapters in the UK literature.

The authors of this book, Dr Richard Austen-Baker, my colleague at Lancaster University Law School, and Dr George Zhou of the School of Law at the University of Leeds, together form a highly suitable team for the writing of a book of this purpose and content. Leaving aside their accomplishments as doctrinal contract scholars, they bring particular expertise to the exposition of the theories discussed in this book. Dr Austen-Baker has made some fine contributions to the development of the relational theory of contract, contributions that I know from personal communication that the late Ian Macneil held in high regard. Amid the general barrenness of law and economics in the UK, Dr Zhou has valuably brought some of the sophistication of the better US contributions to bear on the discussion of issues in the contract law of England and Wales.

I myself have tried to utilise the theoretical insights Dr Austen-Baker and Dr Zhou describe in this book in my own work on contract. I am very happy to see this effort continue in the hands of two members of a subsequent generation of contract scholars who have so ably taken on what, in the end, is the most important task, which I have completely shirked in my own written work, of making those insights of interest to students. I believe Dr Austen-Baker and Dr Zhou have accomplished this task, and have done doing so while conveying the intellectual quality of those insights.

I wish their effort every success.
David Campbell
Lynesack, County Durham
February 2014

Table of cases

United States

Table of UK legislation

Table of international legislation

Table of statutory instruments

Note to students

This book introduces you to just some of the fascinating background to the often rather dry and technical contract law you study in the classroom and library.

Human beings have been making promises to one another and agreements with one another for many thousands of years. Some of these are express ones and others are implicit, built into the very fabric of society. For instance, in the hunter-gatherer village, the potter understands that he must supply pots to the hunters and gatherers, who, in turn, know that the condition for getting the pots they need is supplying meat and berries and nuts to the potter. They all know that the conditions for mutual security include obedience to the decisions of the headman. Some of these exchanges and understandings we would today characterise as a contract in the lawyer's sense, while others we would not. Yet they all involve some sense of an exchange and some sense of a regulated exchange – like a contract or a tax, but unlike a bank robbery. In this book, we do not always suppose that a contract is an agreement that a lawyer or a judge would recognise as a contract, but it will be understood to be at least a regulated exchange.

Several thousand years ago, Babylonian rulers were setting up stone columns, called 'steles', laying down the rules by which people must trade with each other or by which they can sell houses or hire labour. These *steles* may or may not have encompassed the first written codes of contract *law* (they are merely the earliest ones of which we are so far aware). Contract precedes contract law as a human phenomenon, but at least in the scale of sophistication of society, if not in the scale of an absolute number of years, contract law – whether written down or not – must have followed fairly close on the recognition of a concept of the regulated exchange.

This book looks at the purposes of contract as a phenomenon and then of contract law before turning to look at the long history of contract law. We then turn to look at the development of what today, in the common law world at least, we recognise as the law of contract, before considering certain (but by no means all) theoretical concepts that aim to provide a context for the understanding of contracts and the law governing them. We have aimed at being comprehensible rather than comprehensive and at helping you obtain an understanding of what we are talking about – some of which is pretty advanced stuff – rather than merely providing material for you to learn and regurgitate in an examination, much like the parrot learning to say 'Who's a pretty boy, then?'

Unless your contract law course is a very unusual one, you will not find that the chapters of this book fit neatly alongside any of the topics you are studying as the contract syllabus unfolds. It is in the nature of an overview. We suggest you just read it and reflect either before studying contracts, or while studying them, or afterwards before revision, with the hope of understanding it all better and more fully.

Richard Austen-Baker, Lancaster
Qi Zhou, Leeds
February 2014

Note to lecturers

This book is somewhat different from most other books designed as supplementary reading for students of the law of contracts. It does not follow the syllabus by topics – no chapters on agreement, consideration, remedies and so forth. Rather, it sets out to explain the background to contract law: What are contracts for? What is contract law for? How did the modern action for breach of contract develop? It also offers some theoretical approaches: classical/neo-classical contract; realism and formalism; consumer-welfarism and market-individualism; relational contract theory; law and economics.

In discussing all these areas, this book sets out to *explain*. It is not a *textbook* attempting more-or-less comprehensive coverage of the subject matter of each chapter. Rather, the intention is to give an outline that will be sufficient for most students to have a reasonable notion of the subject matter, be it the historical development of contract or, say, legal realism. Neither is it a *primer*. A student who has read, say, Chapter 5 ('The relational context of contract'), will not then be able to trot out the names of half a dozen major authors on relational contract, with a ready quotation or two for each. However, s/he will, the authors sincerely hope, understand what the theory actually *is*, and understand how it might be valued and used by the scholar for its explanatory power and perhaps by the practitioner seeking to design optimal contractual relations for a client.

This book is intended to be readily accessible to the first year law student, since in most university law schools of the common law world at least, contract law tends to be taught in the first year. Bearing in mind that the core demands on the newly minted law student in terms of reading textbooks, cases, legislative material, let alone scholarly articles recommended to them, are already quite considerable, even highly able students may be reluctant to plough through a dense and scholarly book recommended for supplementary reading. For this reason, this book has been written with relative informality and a minimum of detailed citation and quotation. The authors have set out to pass on to the target readership a basic understanding of what are typically regarded as rather advanced topics. The topics are presented in a simple way because the authors do not aim to satisfy the requirements of the advanced student – just the typical beginner.

Lastly, by departing from the approach of discussing substantive contract law topic by topic, where the law may vary somewhat from one jurisdiction to another and possibly very markedly between common law and non-common law jurisdictions, it is hoped that this book will be interesting and relevant to students in *any* jurisdiction.

1 What is contract for?
And what is contract law for?

- What is '(a) contract'?
- The purposes of contract:
  - enterprise
  - power
  - peace
  - chance
- The purposes of contract *law*

What is (a) contract?

You will first notice we have used the classic technique of the academic poseur of sticking one part of a heading or title in brackets. There is a good reason for this here, however. If you ask most people 'what is a contract?', the answer will quite likely be something to do with a long document in small print with signatures at the bottom. If you ask them 'what is contract?', you would probably get much the same answer, as they will have supplied the 'a' for themselves, because they will also be thinking of 'contract' as a concrete 'thing'. But contract is a concept rather than a thing. A contract may be a thing, but is also definitely a concept. We make contracts every day, usually many times. One of the authors of this book used to be the admissions tutor for his law school. Speaking to groups of would-be law students and their parents about studying law, he opened this talk with 'well, I see you all got here today and are all wearing clothes', the first being a remark about criminal and property law (they still have *their* cars, because they have not been taken in the night by someone else, thanks to the concept of private property and the threatened sanctions of criminal law), the second about contract law, because the fact of clothes is the result of an amazingly huge series of contracts: they bought them from a shop in a contract; the shop bought them from the manufacturer in a contract; they travelled from manufacturer to the shop by a series of carriage of goods contracts; they were manufactured in a factory by workers with employment contracts; the shop and the factory had leases, contracts with electricity suppliers; the factory had to buy or lease machinery and had to buy cloth, which had to be produced in a mill, which had to pay rent and have employment contracts and have a contract with a bank (like all the others), all those employees need contracts to buy or rent their houses, buy food, buy electricity, and so on, and so on, and so on. The web of contracts required to put a pair of jeans on a sixth former is absolutely astonishing.

We may also use the *concept* of contract more widely. For instance, there have been 'home-school contracts',[1] which are not contracts that a judge would recognise and enforce; and there is also the notion of a 'social contract' between government and governed.[2]

A good 'legal' definition of a contract, at any rate a popular and enduring one, is that it is 'a promise or set of promises for the breach of which the law provides a remedy'.[3] This is a good definition in some ways and a very problematic one in other ways.

The advantages of such a definition are that:

• It is simple and neat.
• It is a 'lawyerly' definition since a lawyer would recognise it and accept it as at least reasonable and as excluding things people call contracts but which a lawyer would not attempt to enforce as a contract (e.g., 'home-school contracts').
• It is self-validating, because if a court recognises an agreement as a contract then it is enforceable but if it does not recognise it as enforceable then it is nt really a contract at all, so not enforcing it does not offend the idea of 'sanctity of contract' and no example of an agreement being enforced by a court as a contract can invalidate the definition.

The disadvantages of such a definition are that:

• It raises more problems than it solves; for instance, what is being promised? Is a party promising to do the thing stipulated (e.g., deliver a case of wine, work for a law firm, perform at Elton John's birthday party) or simply promising to compensate the other party for any legally recognised loss she or he may suffer if the stipulated thing is not done?

1 These are documents introduced some time ago in English state-funded schools, between schools and parents whose children have been problematic: ill behaved, truanting etc. They have no legal status as they lack requirements for enforceability, notably 'consideration' (a *quid pro quo* recognised by the law – every contract textbook for a common law jurisdiction will have one or more chapters dealing with this).
2 J.-J. Rousseau, *Du Contrat Sociale ou Principes du Droit Politique* (1762). Rousseau argued that the right of a government to legislate depended on a social contract with the people, not on the divine right of kings.
3 Restatement of Contract, s.1 (1932).

- It could be argued that it privileges the notion of 'promise' over that of 'reliance': some people argue that the law of contract is not about enforcing promise keeping but about protecting people from any negative consequences of relying on a promise if that promise were to be broken (more on this in Chapter 3).
- It is extremely narrow in that it privileges a lawyer's definition over other possible definitions that might have more validity in different contexts (e.g., a conventional exchange of gifts might involve a sense of mutual obligation that is, socially, as binding as any contract enforced by a court, also we have the notion of a 'social contract' already mentioned; and what of, for instance, the 'contract of marriage'?). If we are to understand contract as a phenomenon we need to look at a wider canvas than doctrinally limited lawyers' definitions.
- It is self-validating and essentially circular: Q. 'What is a contract?' A. 'A contract is what a judge will enforce as a contract.' Such a definition clearly does not help us to predict judicial action in any given case. Thus, although a lawyer would recognise and assent to it, it does not actually help a lawyer in doing his or her job of predicting what a court would do in any given case.

This rather narrow definition, then, neat as it seems, appears on closer inspection to raise more problems than it solves. All we can really do with it is to say that when a judge says 'this is a binding contract and I'm going to uphold it by awarding damages for breach' then whatever it is to which he refers is a contract.

So, can we find an alternative and more satisfactory definition? This is also problematic. First, it depends on why we want a definition. There are, we suggest, two main reasons we would want a definition. One we might call the 'professional reason'; the other might be called the 'social science reason'. By 'professional reason', we mean that we want a definition so that we can define a contract for the purposes of professional advice: we can advise someone whether an agreement or transaction into which they have entered will be recognised and enforced as a contract by the authorities (the courts) or advise them on what necessary steps to take to ensure that a proposed transaction will be recognised and enforced as a contract by the authorities. By 'social science reason' we mean that we wish to be able to define contracts so that we can identify them for the purposes of studying the rôle (and status and perception and so on and so forth) of contracts in society; contracts as a phenomenon of human interaction.

Ironically, the definition given earlier, which appeared in the purely professional context of the Restatement of Contracts, works (to some extent at least) as a social science definition but is utterly hopeless as a professional definition. We have already seen why it is hopeless for professional purposes. It works as a social science definition, however, because it describes a phenomenon and we can say 'let us study what people do about contracts –

we shall define contracts as "promises or sets of promises which the law recognises as binding and for breach of which the courts provide a remedy" – now let's apply for that research grant.'

Whether it really is adequate as a social science definition is quite another matter: one might argue that there are many human interactions or transactions that share fundamental characteristics with legally enforceable contracts yet which are not themselves enforceable as contracts (and some which are not even labelled loosely as contracts) and that in order to understand contracts in their correct perspective we need to include these other sorts of 'contract', too. Here we are thinking of such things as the 'social contract', the 'contract of marriage' as well as all sorts of other relationship that are more or less like contracts when one comes to look at them. For instance, a friend gives me a birthday present: am I not effectively obliged to buy her one in turn even though we have never agreed anything about it, no court would interfere and our friends would not use the language of contract? The language of contract may be absent but there is a sort of socially, morally and emotionally enforced reciprocity expected in this instance; is that not, for most practical purposes, as much a binding obligation, a contract, as one that a court would enforce? Especially given that the vast majority of proper, legal, contracts will never be enforced in a court, even if breached, since few parties wish to go to that extreme. So what is meant by contract for social science purposes is pretty much infinitely contestable, so we are probably better off asking ourselves whether any given definition works as a social science definition for the particular purpose for which we wish to use it.

As to a professional definition, this is just as difficult. The biggest problem might even be what is our definition of 'definition'? When we think of the word 'definition' we tend to think of something a few words or at most a few sentences long. But perhaps we should be prepared for something a few hundred thousand words long, in which case we can point to, say, *Corbin on Contracts* or Treitel's *Law of Contract* as definitions of contract. The Restatements of Contract would also work. These tell us what will be enforced as contracts and how, and they assist us (in theory at least – and in practice most of the time) to predict whether an agreement or promise will be treated as a contract by a relevant official and, in that case, what they might do about any given behaviour in relation to that agreement or promise. What is taught in law schools as 'the law of contract' is in reality what is also called 'the general theory of contracts' (or 'classical general theory'). This has its origin in the attempt to identify sufficient common points in all contracts and their treatment by the courts to be able to lay down a set of general principles applicable irrespective of the subject matter of any given contract. We will learn more about this in Chapter 3. For now, perhaps, this is enough: we have at least, we hope, sown the seeds of doubt and confusion in our readers' minds, which are a necessary prelude to an exploration of the complexity of the many contexts of contract.

The purposes of contract

So, scurrying red-facedly away from the attempt to define contract, can we say anything about the purposes of contract? Here, we think, we probably can say something rather more useful than we can say in our attempts at definition. The problem of professional definition is by and large irrelevant to this question, since we are asking a question about the social phenomenon that is the activity of contracting. If, for the sake of argument, we adopt the following definition: 'a contract is a relationship recognised and sanctioned in some way by law or custom or social pressure wherein people make or promise some sort of exchange that is at least susceptible of having some economic or social value or function', which may not suit for all purposes but will do for many, we can now go on to make some observations about why we do this making contracts thing.

We do not intend to be the least bit original about this. In 1961 Harold Havighurst gave the Rosenthal Lectures at Northwestern University in America. His lectures were published later that year as *The Nature of Private Contract*[4] and include a fine discussion of the purposes for which we make contracts, which Havighurst calls 'uses' of contract. He is speaking of 'contract-in-fact', that is to say, contracts 'divorced from its legal aspects'.[5] (We shall see whether this is really true, even really possible.) He identifies four such 'uses': enterprise, power, peace and chance. Havighurst, though a reasonably distinguished scholar in his day, is not particularly renowned today and we do not intend to suggest that he is some sort of 'key' or 'canonical' theorist of contract, but his analysis of the purposes of contract seems to the authors of this book to be elegant and attractive and to do as well as any, so for this reason we will devote this section to his fourfold analysis.

Let's take each in turn.

Enterprise

We have to start by considering what 'enterprise' means in the particular concept we are going to use it. Like many words, it has multiple meanings, but fundamental to the academic 'enterprise' is the right to have words mean whatever we say they mean: Humpty Dumpty was clearly a scholar![6] Havighurst here uses enterprise in a very wide, but entirely proper (as a quick glance at a decent dictionary will show), sense of the word:

---

4 H.C. Havighurst, *The Nature of Private Contract* (Northwestern University Press: Chicago, IL, 1961).
5 Ibid., p.10.
6 ' "When *I* use a word," Humpty Dumpty said, in rather a scornful tone, "it means just what I choose it to mean – neither more nor less".' L. Carroll, *Through the Looking Glass and What Alice Found There* (Macmillan: London, 1871), p.72.

Enterprise, as I use the term, includes every kind of project from the most exalted to the most humble. It may be a far-flung operation such as the fighting of a war or the production of goods for a world market; it may be a modest task such as bringing up a family or putting a meal on the table. It may be for profit or not for profit, for an idealistic or a criminal purpose. When the term is so defined, it is difficult to think of any human activity that is not referable to one enterprise or another.[7]

Havighurst goes on to say that contract plays two rôles in enabling enterprise:[8]

- obtaining cooperation of others
- securing protection.

Obtaining cooperation

Most 'enterprises' need some sort of involvement from other people. Bringing up a family, for instance, requires some cooperation from the children, from a spouse or partner we hope, from teachers. We need to put a roof over the family's head requiring the cooperation of a landlord or else of a bank for a mortgage, maintenance and repair people, electricity suppliers and so forth. If we set up a business we need premises – landlords again – working capital, perhaps from a bank, we will likely need to source stock or raw materials, we may need someone to carry out deliveries and we may need employees or partners to work in the business. Here are a series of what might be characterised as 'exchange relations'.

What defines these relations, though? How do we know what to expect from each other? By what means are they regulated? This is where *promises* come in: we make a series of promises to each other; we *exchange* promises. You promise to deliver flour to my bakery when I require it; I promise to pay for it within a certain time and by a certain means: cooperation achieved.

This explanation works well provided our definition of *contract* is wide enough to encompass all promises. Certainly, contracts can help obtain cooperation, e.g., in employing a nursemaid to help bring up a family; but getting one's eldest child to collect a younger sibling from school, for example, involves promise without involving a contract that a court or a lawyer would recognise as such. If we imagine a world without *contract*, we can still have a good deal of cooperation achieved through *promise*. So what is special about contract in obtaining cooperation in enterprise? We want to say here 'security', but Havighurst uses this in a different sense, which we will be moving on to shortly, so, to avoid confusion, we will use the term 'enforceability' to mean the quality that contract adds to promise.

7 Havighurst, op. cit., p.21.
8 Ibid., pp.21–22.

What do we mean by enforceability? We mean here that the State will, if asked, deploy its power to enforce a promise that is enforceable. We mean to distinguish between enforceability and 'bindingness', since promises may be binding in a variety of ways that have nothing to do with enforceability:

- individual conscience or personal ethical imperative
- particular self-interest ('only if I keep this promise to John will John keep his promises to me')
- general self-interest ('if I break my promise to John and other people find out, they might not be prepared to accept my promises themselves and thus not cooperate with me in future')
- image consciousness ('I like other people to think well of me, but if I break my promise to John and they find out, they might think badly of me instead')
- self-image ('I am the sort of person who always keeps his word')
- social pressure (where friends and family start cold shouldering the promisebreaker)
- religious belief ('promises are sacred, bad things might happen to me or my soul if I break this promise').

Doubtless readers can think of others besides these. All of these are factors that can make a promise effectively binding, but in relation to the vast majority of promises, only contract has this quality of enforceability.[9] (We mean, of course, *legal* enforceability; the potential for enforcement by State power: there is also non-State power, such as Big Joe sending the boys round with baseball bats. Promises to Big Joe are also enforceable, but the enforceability in this instance is not *legal* enforceability. We also mean here private promises: promises may be made between States and enforced by quite other means, for example, war.) Contract allows us to *trust* other people's promises of cooperation, allowing us to build the cooperative web that is essential to enterprise. As enterprises grow larger in scale or scope, they grow more complicated and an ever-greater number of reliable promises are required, which are likely to come from more and more people who are less and less likely to be affected in their actions by operating factors such as self-image or social pressure.

That greater numbers of promises are required with more complex enterprises is obvious. Why are the promisors less likely to be affected by factors like self-image and social pressure, though? This becomes obvious with a simple example: I offer to sell you my motor car, delivery of the car to be immediate

---

9 There are other legal principles that may enforce certain promises, such as trusts or some types of estoppel but the number of instances of promises gaining enforceability from these is small by comparison with contract and often they are not concerned with deliberate, express promising at all.

but payment in 10 instalments. If I do not have other means of enforcement (of the Big Joe kind) available to me, how do I know you will not simply drive off and break your promise to pay me? If you are my brother, that may be more unlikely to be a problem, because your conscience, your self-image as a good brother, social pressure from other family and friends, and so on, will make it highly likely that you will, in fact, make the payments. If you are a stranger, then you may not feel the same prickings of conscience, you may find it easier to get over self-image problems and you are not subject to social pressure from my family and friends. For this reason, I want our agreement to be legally enforceable. If it is not, then I will probably not want to take the chance of letting you have my car and, if I am in the car-selling business, or you wish to use the car as a taxicab, for instance, enterprise has been diminished and held back by my unwillingness to cooperate with you in this way.

Having said all this, though, it must not be forgotten that there are other (quite legitimate and extensive) ways of securing cooperation, such as command (which might be governmental as in a socialist State's command economy or indeed government power in any political system, but which might be more private – a parent securing a child's cooperation by command, for example), status obligations (e.g., a physician's professional ethical obligation to treat a person who is not his or her patient, in a medical emergency), religious structures (obedience of a religious group to a priest of some sort, a woman's subjection of herself to her husband in a fundamentalist Christian or Muslim family), fealty to a lord in a feudal society, and so on. Contract is one among a number of ways of securing cooperation, but it is the one that works in nearly every society when we wish to cooperate at arms' length with parties not otherwise specially bound to us.[10]

Securing protection

When Havighurst used this term, he meant not the kind of security we have been discussing earlier, where the existence of a contract and a legal system to enforce it gives us a feeling of security, but rather contracts that are specifically there to bring other parties in to provide security or 'protection' for our enterprise. The idea of a contract for 'protection' will be familiar to Big Joe: it may be a significant part of his business. Trader pays 'protection

---

10 In his discussion of power (see next section), Havighurst mentions Mises' division of social cooperation into two types: 'co-operation by virtue of contract and co-ordination, and co-operation by virtue of command and hegemony' (L. von Mises, *Human Action: A Treatise on Economics* (Yale University Press: New Haven, CT, 1949) p.196, cited by Havighurst at p.28) but we can see here that it is not quite as simple a division as that makes it sound, as, although doubtless with some violence to the ordinary sense of words, all of these examples could somehow be made to fit one or other category.

11 Havighurst, p.25.

money' to Big Joe and Big Joe undertakes that his men will not burn Trader's business premises to the ground or smash the place up. Typically also, Big Joe will put his prestige behind the idea that Big Al, Big Mo and Ma Green should not allow their men to treat Trader's business in this way either. This is sometimes called a contract of *appeasement*.[11]

The obvious legitimate instance is the contract of insurance. Unlike Big Joe, an insurer does not undertake that it will not send someone round to burn the premises down; rather, it promises, in exchange for payment of 'insurance premiums', that if for any reason (other than Trader's deliberate arson) the premises burn down, it will pay agreed sums that may extend to rebuilding, restocking with goods and possibly lost revenue while the business cannot trade.

'The lawsuit and various forms of economic, social and verbal pressure are recognized as legitimate weapons', Havighurst says,[12] before going on to enumerate some examples of how such threats may be guarded against by contracts:

> [H]e may settle lawsuits and strikes, he may obtain from a neighbouring property owner a covenant not to use the land in a way that will adversely affect the enterprise; he may exact from one who sells him a business a covenant not to compete; he may require an employee to give a covenant not to enter a competing business upon the termination of the employment.[13]

Power

In connection with this, Havighurst observes that '[i]n two respects contract has to do with power, and in both there is a close relationship to its use in the achievement of co-operation for the enterprise'.[14]

These two respects are:

* power of the parties in relation to non-parties
* power of one party over the other.

The first may seem odd. After all, non-parties can neither sue *nor be sued* on a contract.[15] But the power here is the power to affect our world that cooperation

---

12 Ibid.
13 Ibid., p.26. It is probably worth noting here, however, that the last example is often somewhat frowned on by courts, especially in relation to typical employees as opposed to top-level staff, as it is often seen as an unfair restraint of trade. There are clearly issues of simple social justice involved in preventing an employee from selling his labour to someone else on leaving, so courts in most common law jurisdictions place strict limitations on the geographic and temporal scope of such covenants.
14 Ibid., 27.
15 Known as the 'doctrine of privity of contract'.

can give us. Havighurst cites the obvious example of the boycott.[16] Agreeing to band together can give a group power over another person or group by making things difficult for them: in the original boycott, Irish tenants demanding a 25 per cent rent reduction refused any communication with the estate manager, Captain Charles Boycott, forcing him to bring in workers for the harvest from Ulster with troops to guard them. More recent examples include British students' boycotts of the products of Nestlé (demanding the company stop selling baby milk formula in Africa) and of Barclays Bank (demanding it withdraw from South Africa during the apartheid era). Actually, none of these instances achieved the desired result, so perhaps the boycott was not such a great example to pick. But a strike, for example, or economic sanctions are really sorts of boycott. Of course, none of these involves legally recognised contracts, but they do fall within the wider definition Havighurst adopted for the purpose of considering contracting as a human behaviour. Groups might, however, contract together to buy more effectively and cheaply, which would be both legally contractual and an effective exercise of power of a sort. Pressure group politics is an area of growth in which groups seek to influence government by banding together and since many of these are membership groups with rules and subscriptions, these are often genuinely and legally contractual networks.

The question of contract conferring power on one party over another is more difficult, we think. The fact of a law of contract does, of course, confer power on contracting parties: if we have a legally binding contract instead of a mere promise, then in addition to any social sanctions, the pressure of your conscience and so on, I am able to threaten and actually invoke the coercive power of the State to put you in a position where you must either perform or suffer consequences designed to put me in as good a position (or as close as remedies can get to doing that) as I would have been in had you performed. The State can use strong-arm methods to force its will on you: sending in bailiffs to seize and sell your goods, selling up your house, even (in the case of a breach of an injunction against breach of contract or a decree of specific performance) carrying you off to gaol. But Havighurst was writing about 'contract in fact', which, as we have seen, goes far beyond actual legally enforceable contracts.

If a non-legally enforceable 'contract' is to give one person power over another, then we must invoke other means of enforcement. X might have power over Y, owing to a 'contract' (whether or not legally enforceable) because X is thereby enabled to oblige Y to do something (which Y will generally have agreed to). But the enforcement may be by social pressure or familial expectation or market forces, as discussed already. Then there are the power imbalances created by legislation, necessity and trickery or fraud (we are using 'trickery' to refer to activity that is not actually criminal or even

16 Ibid.

unlawful in many jurisdictions but which distorts decision making by one party). In Britain and many other countries, it is forbidden to drive a motorised vehicle on public roads without having liability insurance to cover claims by other people who may be harmed by your bad driving. Legislation forces all of us who wish to drive to make contracts with insurance companies, which gives them considerable power. For a start, these policies are pretty much on a 'take it or leave it' basis; we might well have a certain amount of choice about features (how much excess[17] we have to pay in the event of a claim; whether we are absolutely entitled to a 'courtesy car' while our car is being repaired, etc.), but most of the terms are laid down by the insurer and are not negotiable and these terms are unlikely to differ very much from one motor insurer to another. Moreover, the insurer gets a lot of other power over the insured: drive too fast and get a speeding ticket, to cite one among many factors, and the insurer may increase the price of renewal or even refuse to renew. As to necessity, as Lord Northington LC put it in *Vernon v Bethell*, 'necessitous men are not, truly speaking, free men.'[18] What he really meant is that a person in an exceptionally poor bargaining position, requiring something necessary to his existence and obliged to take such terms as are on offer, does not really enter into a contract freely: he has a choice between agreeing to the terms and, perhaps, starving or freezing.

In recent years, shareholders of any British bank, surveying the quarterly financial reports and noting the amount having to be set aside to compensate customers who were 'mis-sold' payment protection insurance (PPI), will have a very real and personal understanding of the notion of trickery or fraud. Those same banks have also been involved in various other scams to pick the pockets of their customers. The customers are advised to take out some product, such as PPI, the detailed terms of which are not explained to them and if they were, would need for all but the sophisticated consumer a proper explanation of how the risks affect them in their particular situation. The product is so designed that it is unlikely to pay out and is often sold to those never likely to need it anyway and at a price grossly inflated compared with its cost to the bank (in the case of PPI, something like 500 per cent above cost). A similar example is the extended warranty on consumer durables such as refrigerators, cookers or televisions. These days such products are highly unlikely to break down and are mostly not that expensive to repair, or simply replace, especially compared with the price charged for the warranty, which often costs enough (to the consumer) over three or four years to pay for a replacement. The cost to the retailer is typically a minute fraction of the amount charged to the consumer (perhaps as little as a one-off premium of a couple of pounds for a warranty for which the consumer will pay the retailer, over three years, in the order of £150 to £200).[19] The examples of this sort of thing are so numerous that we

17 Known in some countries as 'deductible'.
18 (1761) 2 Eden 110 at 113.

could probably fill a multivolume work with describing them before we ever get to an example of one that actually amounts to a legally recognised fraud. We have said enough, we think, for the reader to have a good idea of what we are getting at.

Peace

The most obvious example of making agreements, or 'contracts' for peace is the peace treaty: two or more countries agreeing together to cease armed conflict and/or not to engage in armed conflict in the future. But these are not, of course, private contracts or agreements. In the private sphere, we might cite the 'protection racket' as an instance: 'Pay me money and my men will refrain from beating you up, burning your premises down and so on and I will use my force and prestige to prevent any other criminal gang doing likewise.' That, of course, is not a lawful contract as only the State is entitled to threaten physical force if we do not hand over our money (i.e., our taxes). However, there are plenty of lawful examples of private contracts for peace. The most significant for most lawyers is the compromise ('settlement') of lawsuits. Such agreements are valid and enforceable contracts,[20] the consideration on either side being the sacrifice of a chance of outright victory in court, and this is true even where one side's case is weak, provided that it is not the case that one side has no case and knows that he has no case.[21] Another example like this one is the settlement of a labour dispute in order to have industrial peace. (Although in English law, the outcome of collective bargaining is not enforceable as a contract,[22] while it is in some other jurisdictions.[23])

19 One of the authors caused raised eyebrows at a conference of English and US contract jurists when he said that only an idiot would take out extended warranties, but the raised eyebrows were all among the American delegates, many of whom had apparently taken such extended warranties, so it may be that either the economics of such warranties are very different in America or else that they were thinking of extended warranties on motor cars, which is a very different proposition altogether, even in England.

20 In some jurisdictions, there may be exceptions to this; certainly in England, settlements of financial matters in divorce cases are by no means always recognised as final and binding until confirmed by a judge in the form of a consent order.

21 *Callisher v Bischoffsheim* (1870) LR 5 QB 449, *Attorney-General of British Columbia v The Deeks Sand & Gravel Company Ltd* [1956] SCR 336 (Canada), *Wahl v Barnum* 116 N.Y. 87 (1889) (USA), *Hercules Motors Pty Ltd v Schubert* [1953] SR (NSW) 301 (Australia), for example.

22 In English common law, such agreements were *prima facie* not regarded as intended to create legal relations: *Ford Motor Co. Ltd v AEF* [1969] 1 WLR 339. Under the Trade Union and Labour Relations (Consolidation) Act 1992 (UK) such an agreement is 'conclusively presumed' not to be intended to create legal relations unless it is in writing and expressly provides that it is intended to be a legally enforceable contract (s.179(1) and (2)).

23 Germany being a prime instance.

There are other examples that are less obviously contracts for peace, in large part because peace is only one of the functions or uses of the contract in question (for instance, a country's armed forces buying weapons from an arms manufacturer). This is a contract for peace in the sense that the country wishes to arm itself effectively to deter other countries or internal opponents from attempting an attack, but for the arms manufacturer, the use of contract here is enterprise rather than peace; for the country itself there is clearly also an intention to use the contract to give it power, in a very raw and obvious sense.

Chance

Havighurst's final 'use' is chance. He comes to this somewhat reluctantly because, although he acknowledges that all contracts involve some element of chance,[24] in treating chance as one of the uses of contract he was considering contracts deliberately made for chance, that is to say gambling, something rather disapproved of in the early 1960s. It is supposed that these contracts are made for enjoyment, but, of course, some people gamble in the hope of making a profit. In that case, one could also include millions of contracts made every day, indeed every hour, on financial, stock, commodity and other markets, few of which are intended as investments in enterprises, the vast majority of which are mere bets on expected price changes. Of course, genuine enterprising contracts involve an element of chance but they are not pure gambling, whereas buying oil futures with no interest in ever getting any oil, only the hope of selling the future later in the day for a higher price than you paid clearly is the same as gambling; the mere fact that there may be some skill involved does not change that, because many gambling games, particularly card games, involve elements of skill, as does, for instance, judging the form of a horse to bet on in a horserace. Since many thousands of people make a considerable living out of gambling on behalf of investment banks, and jobs working for such institutions are widely seen as prestigious and highly desirable, we must see chance as a 'respectable' use of contract.

The purposes of contract *law*

We can put this very briefly, so we shall. We are clear that there are many factors that cause contracts (or promises) to be kept: mere shared interest in the positive outcome of the thing agreed on; social pressure; morality; religion and so on. However, when dealing at arms' length, we tend to crave additional security. This can be achieved by, for instance, hostage taking or some equivalent (for instance, leaving a valuable item with a pawnbroker as a

---

24 Op. cit., p.40.

'pledge' to assure repayment of a loan). More practical in most cases is the assurance that the power of the State can be brought to bear to compel performance or at least monetary compensation regarded as reasonably equivalent to performance. The law provides that enforceability and the conditions under which a contract will be enforced and how. Furthermore, contract law provides a considerable amount of content for contracts: for instance, implied terms. Contract law may also be used by the State to regulate contractual activity, often to limit the exercise of power of one party over another (for example, in Britain there is the Unfair Contract Terms Act 1977, which regulates the use of limitation and exclusion clauses, which are typically deployed by parties in stronger bargaining positions; in the EU generally there is the Unfair Terms in Consumer Contracts Directive and the various national legislation putting it into effect, which places considerable restrictions on unduly burdensome terms in take-it-or-leave-it consumer contracts). Finally, contract law, by refusing to enforce some contracts (e.g., contracts facilitating prostitution, in some jurisdictions gambling contracts, contracts for the sale of illegal things like narcotic drugs), signals society's disapproval of some activity, even where that activity is not actually prohibited by law (e.g., in England prostitution itself is not illegal).

Suggested further reading

P.S. Atiyah, 'The Modern Role of Contract Law', in *Essays on Contract* (Oxford University Press: Oxford, 1986).

H.C. Havighurst, *The Nature of Private Contract* (Northwestern University Press: Chicago, IL, 1961).

2 The historical context of contract

- Ancient contract law
- Medieval contract law
- The rise of the action of *assumpsit*
- Pothier and mutual assent
- Judicial innovation in the nineteenth century
- 'Leading cases' and the textbook tradition
- The rise of 'legal realism'

Ancient contract law

Our earliest human ancestors were 'hunter-gatherers'. That is, people who survived by hunting animals (and presumably fishing) and by gathering berries, nuts, roots and so on. They left no written record of their way of life, so we are left speculating as to how they lived. It has generally been accepted as reasonable to suppose that initially each of these people did everything for himself, or at least within a family unit. They hunted and made for themselves the means of hunting. When fire was discovered, they gathered wood and made sparks. When first they made vessels for cooking and storage, each would make his or her own. At some point, however, our ancestors came to specialise. This was a very important step. It is the basis of human civilisation. Someone who is good at hunting focuses on hunting and shares the meat he gets with someone who is good at making arrowheads and someone else who is good at making pots. As soon as this type of exchange occurred we needed understandings about exchange. Probably before then we needed some understandings: we see even in animals a tendency to share the fruits of successful hunting with those who have been less fortunate (vampire bats provide a fine example) with no doubt an expectation that when fortunes are reversed the same courtesy will be extended in return. But with specialisation the need becomes much more pressing and more complex, because one person may make exchanges with several others. Eventually whole communities may become to some extent specialised and need to trade with other communities that have specialised in other things. The need for very clear understandings becomes very pressing at this point. Moreover, it may become efficient to have understandings about the terms of trade, for example, one dugout canoe equals 10 buffalo, or whatever.

So, every ancient society, once it developed enough to be called that – indeed as a necessary preliminary to getting to the position to be called a 'society' – must necessarily have developed some sort of way of mediating what we might call commercial disputes. There must have been either some definite understandings that, if breached, would result in community sanctions. We could call this 'substantive' exchange law (i.e., a set of rules of the game, binding on the parties), or else these societies would have needed there to be a person to whom parties could turn if disaffected and whose word was considered in some way binding on the parties. We could describe this latter as an 'adjectival' exchange law (i.e., a binding procedure for settling disputes is laid down). Quite likely they would early on have developed both of these, so that a judge or arbitrator would have emerged whose decision was binding, but he (or perhaps she – early societies seem to have been ruled mainly by women, with 'kings' as consorts or ritual figures only)[1] who was guided in his decisions by accepted rules of the game. Sadly, as noted, they inconsiderately failed to leave behind records of their systems.

The laws of Hammurabi

Humans seem first to have developed really substantial communities around 8,000–10,000 BC, when the earliest 'cities' (really walled villages with some sort of agricultural holdings outside), such as Erech and Ur, came into being in the fertile area between the Tigris and Euphrates rivers known as Mesopotamia, which is located in the modern-day state of Iraq. And it is here that our records begin, since among the shifting alliances and hegemonies in this cradle of civilisation arose Babylon. In time, Babylon had a king called Hammurabi, who came to the throne in around 1792 BC. When Hammurabi came to power in Babylon, it was, in the words of H.W.F. Saggs, 'a well-established but still minor kingdom, no bigger than a small English county, with a radius of about fifty miles'[2] and a vassal state of the Assyrian empire. He left Babylon at the end of his reign a great empire bigger than today's Iraq. The empire is gone, but the 'code' of laws he gave his people remains.

This code was discovered by excavations in Susa, in southwest Iran, in the digging season of 1901–1902, inscribed on *steles* (monumental stones). For a

---

1 See, generally, Sir J. Frazer, *The Golden Bough: A Study in Magic and Religion*, 2nd edn (Macmillan: London, 1900).

2 H.W.F. Saggs, *The Babylonians* (Folio Society: London, 1999), p.63. (Originally published as *The Greatness that was Babylon* in 1962, with a second edition, much revised, appearing in 1988. The Folio edition is a reprint of the 1988 text.)

long while it was the oldest legal code we knew, but since then others that are earlier have been discovered, of which the most significant are:

1   The laws of Ur-Nammu (who was the founder and first king of the Third Dynasty of Ur, the precursor to the state of Sumer, who came to power in 2113 BC), written in Sumerian, of which we have two damaged copies, the texts of which were first published in 1952 and 1965.
2   The laws of Lipit-ishtar, King of Isin, about halfway between the time of Ur-nammu and that of Hammurabi, also written in Sumerian. In this case, we have several fragments of clay tablets, containing the whole or parts of 38 laws.
3   The laws of Eshnunna, found in 1947 at Tell Harmal, now part of Baghdad, consisting of a prologue listing fixed prices, hire rates and wages, and 48 other substantive sections dealing with trespass, loans and interest, marriage, rape and adultery, deflowering of other men's foster mothers, slave girls, personal injury, theft and ownership of slaves, damage by animals or collapsing walls, and illegal divorce.

Hammurabi's code contains a lot of echoes of Eshnunna's, as Moses' code contains striking echoes of Hammurabi's (although this does not mean that Moses was inspired by Hammurabi, rather that there were many common customs in the ancient Near East.) It is, however, much more extensive, or extensively preserved, and more logically arranged than the earlier laws. It is not, however, necessarily an example of legislation as we would understand it today or anything like the modern codes of civilian jurisdictions. As Saggs says:

> The kingdom [Hammurabi] had created, extending from south-west Iran to east Syria, contained a large number of former city-states and petty kingdoms, and although these shared a single culture, there were local variations in customs. [In addition there was a mix of citizens from the old city-states and immigrants of the much more primitive Amorites and] these two groups would have widely conflicting customs. Anyone involved in a legal case would expect to have it settled in accordance with the practice of his own background. But inevitably disputes would arise between two parties . . . with different antecedents, and then a decision would have to be made about which of two different legal practices should prevail. It fell to Hammurabi to make the decisions in such cases, and this is what the laws are and what he called them. They were decisions in particular cases, incorporating principles which Hammurabi had applied in certain actual cases, and which he caused to be recorded as specimen decisions for future comparable cases.[3]

---

3   Saggs, op. cit., pp.172–3.

We think Saggs puts it slightly wrongly as the wording suggests a code on what we call 'conflict of laws' or 'private international law'. The Code of Hammurabi seems to have acted more like a common code accepted to be applicable to multijurisdictional disputes – something like the Vienna Convention. That is to say, since the customs would be multifarious owing to the several different states that had been combined in his kingdom, Hammurabi cannot be laying down a decision as to which of two different customs should be applied. Instead, he is saying, wherever there are divergent customs between the parties, the judges will ignore both and apply this decision instead. The form does resemble in a way the *ratio decidendi* of the modern common law judge, in that a general rule is stated in accordance with which the decision has been made.

The code is generally divided by modern scholars into 282 numbered sections taken direct from the *stele* (stone column) on which the code was inscribed plus sections X, Y and Z. A very large number of these relate to commercial activity that generally involves some sort of contract: employment, bailment (where one person has care of another's moveable property), hire, agency, bonds, credit, debt and so on. The code is not arranged thematically and many sections cross two or more of what would today in most jurisdictions be regarded as distinct areas of law. There are also sections that cross over several areas, as with §.7:

> If a man has bought silver, gold, manservant or maidservant, ox or sheep or ass, or anything whatever its name, from the hand of a man's son, or of a man's slave without witness and bonds, or has received the same on deposit, that man has acted the thief, he shall be put to death.[4]

We would count this really as a criminal law provision, but we also have problems of agency, evidence and title, which are issues in modern law governing transactions, although the 'remedy' is rather unfamiliar in the context of transactional law today. Moreover, §§.66–100 were erased, most likely by a subsequent Elamite conqueror.[5] Sections X, Y and Z belong to these erased columns and the texts of these we have today are taken from Assyrian copies. So it is really not possible to say, 'the following list of sections are "about" contracts'. An example of the provisions made for one type of contract will give the reader a flavour of the code.

---

4 This and all other quotations here from the Code are taken from C.H.W. Johns, *The Oldest Code of Laws in the World: The Code of Laws Promulgated by Hammurabi, King of Babylon B.C. 2285–2242* (T. & T. Clark: Edinburgh, 1903). (More recent scholarship has moved the dates for Hammurabi somewhat closer to the present.)

5 Johns, op. cit, p.ix.

Shepherds' contracts

§.261 If a man has hired a herdsman for the cows or a shepherd for the sheep, he shall give him eight *GUR* of corn per annum.

§.263 If he [the herdsman or shepherd] has caused an ox or sheep which was given to him to be lost, ox for ox, sheep for sheep, he shall render to their owner.

§.264 If a herdsman who has had cows or sheep given him and the shepherd, has received his hire, whatever was agreed, and his heart was contented, had diminished the cows, diminished the sheep, lessened the offspring, he shall give offspring and produce according to the tenure of his bonds.

§.265 If a shepherd to whom cows and sheep have been given him to breed, has falsified and changed their price, or has sold them, one shall put him to account, and he shall render cows and sheep to their owner tenfold what he has stolen.

§.266 If in a sheepfold a stroke of God has taken place or a lion has killed, the shepherd shall purge himself before God, and the accident to the fold the owner of the fold shall face it.

§.264 If a shepherd has been careless and in a sheepfold caused a loss to take place, the shepherd shall make good the fault of the loss which he has caused to be in the fold and shall pay cows or sheep and shall give to their owner.

We see here that the Code takes a mandatory approach to most issues. Wages are clearly a matter for agreement or perhaps more local customs, as evidenced by §.264, notwithstanding §.261 but the legislator has tried otherwise to cover the disputes that will most likely arise and lay down a definite outcome: the parties do not decide between themselves who bears what risk or what shall be the remedy for breach; all of this is prescribed. In that particular sense, it is closer to civilian-style legal systems than to common law systems.

This was obviously not the only source of ancient law, but except for the Romans, it is the only one we have that gives detailed provisions that relate to private contract. A lot of other material we have tends to relate to crimes and particular to religious law. One feature particularly worth noting about Babylonian law in Hammurabi's time is that nearly all contracts had to be in writing (for which clay tablets were used) made before witnesses and sealed with the parties' and witnesses' cylinder seals or, later, marked with the print of thumbnail.[6]

---

6 Saggs, op. cit., p.227.

Roman law

The Romans, as well as being a great warrior people and great imperial administrators, were a highly commercial people. They traded far and wide and delighted in exotic wares. They were fine craftsmen, too. They had, necessarily, a good deal of law governing contracts. But Roman law was rather different in shape from the common law. There were general rules of contract but these contained some startling gaps. For instance, there were rules on duress and on capacity to contract, which applied to contracts of all sorts. But there were no general principles governing formation of contracts such as the rules on offer and acceptance that are universal in common law jurisdictions. The rules on contract formation varied from one type of contract to another as did rules on what we should call 'consideration' and rules relating to remedies.

So, for instance, in most contracts, a promise was enforceable that had been given in exchange for something given or some act performed by the promisee, but the thing had actually to have been given or the act performed or there was no enforceable contract, in sharp contrast with the rule of the common law that there must generally be consideration for any promise we seek to enforce but that it is not the actual doing of the act or giving of the thing that is consideration, rather the *promise* of the act or the thing. Thus, in the common law, the fact that one party has not actually carried out the promise that forms their consideration is no bar to their enforcing the other party's promise, but the value of their own promise, if not performed, will be deducted from the damages paid by the other party. In Roman law, however, in relation to the generality of contracts if A has promised to pay B two sesterces for some service, he cannot sue B for failure to perform unless he, A, has already paid the two sesterces. That rule did not apply, however, to specified categories of contract: 'real' and 'consensual' contracts. In real contracts, there had to have been a delivery under a recognised form of contract, then it would be enforceable. In consensual contracts, like modern common law contracts mere agreement was enough without any actual performance having taken place, to render the contract enforceable. Sales contracts (*emptio venditio*) were instances of this. There is no room in a book like this for a detailed discussion of Roman law on contracts, but there are specialist works you might like to look at, especially if you are from a jurisdiction particularly affected by Roman law models. What to recommend would depend on the jurisdiction in question, so we would suggest that if you want to read more about Roman law from the perspective of your own legal system, you ask your tutor to recommend reading.

Medieval contract law

Medieval law, like so much of the past, is very much 'another country'. We are accustomed today to thinking about the law as a set of principles governing the law's response to certain factual situations. I get run over by a car, so I sue the driver for compensation for my injuries. The problem is one of the law of negligence and the law on quantum of damages for personal injuries. I agree to buy a motor car and we have a question of contract law and of its subset, sales law. To the medieval legal mind, however, these did not mean anything at all (and not just because they did not have motor cars). The medieval legal world was concerned with what we would call procedural law. It was all about getting the right bills and writs, representing the correct forms of action. Find the right form of action and you had a case. If you could not find the right form, well then, you did not have a case.

There is no hope of explaining in just one chapter, let alone a section of one chapter, the complexities of the medieval system or to give a detailed outline of how contract law developed. But we can give you a flavour of medieval law and a rough guide as to how the English courts, their judges and the lawyers who practised in them brought about a workable law of contract that lasted for centuries and left very considerable traces of itself in our law today. In case you doubt the importance of medieval law for today's contract law, bear in mind that the doctrines of consideration and privity, the remedy of damages for lost expectation and the rule against penalties are direct descendants of the medieval law and bear close resemblance in their modern forms to their ancestors.

In considering medieval law, one first needs to remember that there were very many courts. Each local lord had his court. His villeins and dependents could resort to this court for a rough and ready justice between them, although it would be little use if their case were against the lord himself. There were also customary local courts that had derived from the Hundred Moots and Shire Moots that were the bodies administering local government as well as justice. Where there was a fair or market, there would be a court on the day to decide disputes between people at the market – since these dealt with matters on the spot they came to be known as *pied powder* (or 'dusty foot') courts because they dealt with matters while the dust was still on the parties' feet.

The local courts, as we have observed, took in matters of justice along with what was really their main business, that is to say, local government. Administering justice was not seen as being a fundamentally different thing to government. In the same way the king's court, or *Curia Regis*, was merely the presence of the king, with his courtiers, in any given place. His decision as to a dispute or a crime brought before him was simply a part of the business of government and no different from his decision in any other matter affecting his subjects. The justice of the king's court came to be preferred, understandably, to that of local courts as being more reliable and disinterested. The problem was how to get a case decided by the royal court. First, one had to get a writ. This was a thin strip of paper containing a Latin command from the king for something to be done. In the Council and in the Chancery, a case could be begun by bill, but we shall leave that aside for the moment. The right sort of writ was needed in each case. Here it is necessary to understand that, to the medieval mind, there was a definite distinction between a right and a wrong. A right was something perpetual. Establishing a right determined the position of the parties before the court for all time. An instance might be the ownership of land. A wrong, by way of contrast, had already been done and could obviously not be undone. It could be investigated and some sort of remedy or punishment applied far more easily. A wrong was essentially something done that was said to breach someone's 'peace'. Everyone had his 'peace' but the king's peace was held to extend across the land. Only serious wrongs would be brought before the royal courts as breaches of the king's peace, however.

The establishment of a right was a very solemn and complicated process begun by a '*praecipe* writ'. After a very great deal of to-ing and fro-ing, a case brought by *praecipe* writ should technically be decided through trial by battle in the case of a writ of right. The form for a debt (and originally for covenant) was wager of law (oath taking). The form of a *praecipe* writ was to order the sheriff of a county to ensure that a certain act was done (e.g., handing over possession of some land, or else make the person who ought to do it explain why he had not done it). For example:

> The King to the sheriff of Nottinghamshire, greeting. Command ['*Praecipe*'] *A* that justly and without delay he render to *B* one messuage with the appurtenances in *D*, which he claimeth to be his right and inheritance, and to hold of us in chief, and whereof he complains that the aforesaid *A* unjustly deforceth him; and unless he will do this, and [if] the aforesaid *B* shall give you security to prosecute his claim, then summon by good summoners the aforesaid *A* that he be before our justices at Westminster on such a day to show wherefore he hath not done it. And have there the summoners and this writ. Witness, etc.[7]

At first *A* would have had the option of simply handing over the land concerned. If he did not do so then, provided the plaintiff, *B*, could provide proper security for pursuit of the claim, *A* would have to come to Westminster and the case would be determined by the justices. Originally there would have been a trial by battle, but Henry II (1154–1189) was a great reformer and he introduced jury trial as an alternative to battle at the option of the defendant. In course of time the option of simply carrying out the command became a mere fiction so the writ became what we would call 'original process', which is to say that it is the document that starts the case before the courts. After the delivery of the writ there would be many stages before the case would come before the court and although Henry II had set in train modernisation of the legal system, by the time of Edward I (1272–1307) all further reform of

---

7 This translated writ is taken from J.H. Baker, *An Introduction to Legal History*, 2nd edn (Butterworths: London, 1979), p.439. Professor Baker's source was the 1794 edition of Fitzherbert's *Natura Brevium*.

procedure by *praecipe* writ had ground to a halt. For that reason, litigants increasingly looked to other means to pursue their cases.

The obvious choice was the trespass writ. This asserted that a wrong had been done. Wrongs were much less important and solemn than rights. The procedure was quicker, simpler and cheaper. As was also the case for *praecipe* writs, there were specific writs for specific trespasses. Trespass writs involved 'force and arms' (*vi et armis*) and applied both to land and to the person (in the latter case, it is the tort of battery). Lawyers began to use these writs for quite other purposes; for instance, claiming that the plaintiff's horse had been injured by a farrier 'with force and arms' and the *vi et armis* clause became an accepted fiction. But the chancery clerks (to whom litigants in any royal court had to apply for any writ) claimed a right by custom to devise and issue new writs by analogy with existing ones.[8] In the old writs, the *vi et armis* clause was a very general one covering a wide range of wrongdoing. In the new writs, the specific complaint had to be set out. Thus was born 'trespass on the case'; that is to say, an action for trespass brought on the basis of the case stated in the writ. These dealt with a wide range of trespasses that were not committed forcibly. The most obvious example to the student today is the action for negligence.

So far, so 'what's this got to do with contracts?' Contracts were a difficult fit for the medieval legal system. No doubt the vast majority of cases were dealt with reasonably satisfactorily in local courts. In 1215 Glanvill wrote that the royal courts were not concerned with private agreements. But it is clear that there was an increasing desire to litigate private agreements in those courts, even if the reasons for this are not so clear. There were *praecipe* writs to bring contract cases before the royal judges. The action of covenant was an action to oblige a promisor to carry out his promise to the promisee. Generally, it was brought in local courts where proof was by *compurgation* – that is to say each party brought along some other local people to swear to the fact averred by that party. If the agreement were put into a deed, then there was no need to prove the agreement, only the breach. If the agreement were not in a deed then a number of witnesses could be brought to say that the promise had been made, called a 'suit'. So, there could be two 'wagers of law' in the case of an oral covenant: one that the covenant existed at all; the second as to its performance or non-performance. The action could, however, be brought also before the royal courts. At first the royal courts treated these cases on the same basis as the local courts did. However, there were two big problems:

1   *Oath-helpers.* Parties from the country were hardly likely to bring a dozen friends with them all the way to Westminster, days or weeks of hard journeying, to be their oath-helpers. Indeed, they might not even attend

---

8   For a long time this was wrongly thought to be on the basis of the Statute of Westminster II 1285, *In Consimili Casu*, but the practice did not, in fact, begin until 50 years after the statute. If the Chancery clerks thought the statute authorised this then they would have done it sooner rather than resorting to their various tricks and fictions. See Baker, op. cit., p.58.

themselves, but be represented by an attorney (one who acts on another's behalf in any matter). The otherwise unemployed of London would hang around at Westminster Hall and act as oath-helpers for money. This might lead them to be eternally damned for having sworn on the Bible to something that was not true, but it provided ready money in the meantime. From the courts' point of view, however, it made the whole business a complete charade.

2   *Specific performance.* The remedy in covenant was an order that the defendant should carry out his promise, akin to the modern decree of specific performance. This was no use where the defendant had carried out the promise but done it badly – e.g., built a house, as promised, but it is a very poor job with a leaky roof and shaky foundations. It was also no use where the defendant had put performance beyond his power, e.g., a promise by D to convey land to P but D has conveyed it to A instead. D cannot now convey it to P, so the action of covenant provides P with no remedy. If D sold P faulty goods, again there would be no remedy: he had already handed P the goods.

The royal courts dealt with the first problem by, in due course, insisting on a deed to prove the covenant. In the *Case of the Waltham Carrier* at the London eyre of 1321 (86 SS 287), a case was brought against a carrier who covenanted, orally, to take a cartload of hay from Waltham to London. The court refused to accept the case because there was no deed (an agreement in writing with a seal, also called a 'specialty'). Counsel urged that writing was not appropriate for every little promise but Herle J declared that: 'We will not undo the law for a cartload of hay. Covenant is nothing but an agreement between parties in words, but the words can only be proved by specialty.' According to Baker, '[a]fter this, we hear no more of plaintiffs bringing actions of covenant without deeds'.[9] Baker goes on to note that:

> Contemporaries would not have viewed the new common law rule as a drastic denial of justice. True, one could not put every little covenant into writing; but then one should not be able to bother the royal courts with every little unwritten covenant. The restriction applied only in the king's central courts. The local courts in the time of Edward II were quite competent to deal with informal agreements, while royal justice remained available to those with the wisdom and foresight to invest their agreements with the solemnity of parchment and wax. Thus there was no change in the law itself, but only a demarcation of jurisdictions.[10]

The most important agreements were put into deeds but the action of covenant withered anyway because of the development of the 'conditioned bond'. This

9   Ibid., p.265.
10   Ibid., pp.265–266.

was a deed in which A would acknowledge an obligation to pay a given amount of money to B unless he, A, should before a certain date have carried out specified acts. For example, A might promise to pay B the sum of £50 if he did not before next Michaelmas Day build a house for B. If A did build the house (for which there would be a matching obligation to pay), then the bond to pay £50 did not come into effect as the obligation to pay was conditional on not having built a house. If he did not build the house then B would have an action against him on the bond, not in covenant for not building the house, but in debt for the promise to pay £50. Debt was as old an action as covenant and could arise in two ways, either on a contract or on an obligation. In those days a contract meant an actual transaction or act. So if A sells B a sack of corn for a shilling and hands over the corn, then B owes to A one shilling. A mere promise to give a sack of corn to B if B should pay to a shilling to A was not a contract but a covenant. The debt of one shilling arose because of the *quid pro quo* of having handed over a sack of corn. An obligation was a sealed document by which one party acknowledged to any who might read the document that he had bound himself to pay a certain sum to the other party by a given date. This approach allowed the parties to agree to a sum that would be payable to one party should the other fail to carry out his substantive promise, which so far as damages for nonfeasance (not doing something one has promised to do) went, solved the problem of remedies inherent in the action of covenant. However, two problems were left with the law on contracts:

- The Chancery eventually started to relieve against the penal payments due under conditioned bonds.
- There was an action through either covenant or debt for nonfeasance, but neither of these helped in cases of misfeasance (doing something badly).

The first problem never entirely went away; it is with us today as 'the rule against penalties'. The second problem was addressed by use of the action for trespass. If I hurt you or your goods, that is a trespass. But there is an inherent conceptual problem. If I attack you and your horse and hurt the horse, then clearly I am responsible for the hurt to the horse. But what about where you hand me the horse voluntarily so that I can put a new shoe on it? And I injure it not because I mean to hurt it, but by accident? The old writs of trespass probably would not help. There is no general liability to prevent injury to other people and their goods. But the new trespass on the case could do so where someone had negligently carried out their promise to me so as to hurt me or something that is mine because in the making of the promise he has 'taken in hand' (*manucepit*) or undertaken (*assumpsisset*) to achieve a result and instead has done it so badly as to cause me loss or damage. According to Baker,[11] the first

---

11 Op. cit., p.274.

known case in which the superior courts imposed liability in trespass on someone who, having undertaken[12] to do something did it badly causing loss to the plaintiff was the King's Bench case of *Buckton v Tounesende*, known as the *Humber Ferry Case*, in 1348.[13] A bill of trespass was brought alleging that the defendant ferryman accepted the plaintiff's mare to take her across the River Humber, but had overloaded the ferry resulting in the mare's death. Although the defendant's counsel argued that the case should have been brought in covenant (which would have been fatal to the plaintiff's case as covenant did not lie in the King's Bench and also because he almost certainly would not have got the agreement in a deed) the court held that overloading and thereby causing the mare's death was a trespass. This was followed by a variety of cases against surgeons, human and veterinary, which firmly established the principle that where the defendant had promised to do something for the plaintiff and had done it negligently, causing loss or damage, the plaintiff could succeed with a writ of trespass on the case. But so far the cases are really ones that we would recognise today as being as much cases of the tort we now refer to as 'negligence' (really trespass on the case for negligence) as cases of contract. Depending on particular contexts and some jurisdictional differences, one might bring any case of this kind either as a tortious claim or as a claim in contract. The problem still remained of what to do when the proposed defendant had promised to do something but simply had not done it. Nonfeasance rather than misfeasance. Surely where nothing had been done so as to cause harm the claim that the defendant had promised to do something should sound in covenant? A very long period followed in which attempts were made and usually rebuffed. Lawyers tried all sorts of cunning ways around the problem such as relying on the incidences of status – someone promising to look after something made him a bailee, which was a status with certain duties attached and failure to perform would make him liable in *assumpsit*. Similarly, they borrowed from the mercantile courts the idea of warranty of goods. If someone warranted goods to be something they were not then he was guilty of a deceit. There were criminal penalties for this but also a civil action on the case for deceit. (For a detailed account, read Baker, Chapter 16.)

At length, however, a great innovating judge came along in the person of Chief Justice Fyneux who held in Gray's Inn that one who had paid for land could bring *assumpsit* against a seller who failed to deliver seisin (effective possession) of the land and that, on the same principle, a plaintiff could sue a carpenter in *assumpsit* for failure to build a house.[14] This came to be the accepted position; Baker notes that 'there is no reported case in which it was

---

12 The word used in the report of the case was 'emprist' which is French for *assumpsit*, although the official record simply says he 'received to carry safely' (*recepit ad salvo cariandum*).

13 (1348) Kiralfy SB 187; Kiralfy AC 222.

14 Fitz Abr, *Accion sur le Case*, pl. 45.

ever again questioned.'[15] But it is important to note that there had to have been the payment. The plaintiff must have performed his part of the bargain before he could bring an action on the case. If there is no prepayment then the plaintiff would be confined to suing in covenant if he could. In time, however, prepayment became unnecessary, so long as the plaintiff had given something of value to the defendant, which could itself be a promise, 'in consideration' of the defendant's promise for breach of which the plaintiff was now suing. This was because every contract yet to be performed necessarily included a corresponding *assumpsit* to pay anything due in return. So, in *Slade's Case*, D agreed to sell a field to P in exchange for P's promise to pay £16 to D and it was held (by a show of hands in the King's Bench, reversing the decision of the Common Pleas) that the promise to pay £16 created an enforceable right for D to get £16 from P. Thus P had provided a valuable consideration for D's promise to convey the field and could enforce it even though the £16 was not prepaid.[16] Thus was established the right to damages for nonfeasance of a wholly executory (yet to be performed) contract. 'But how is this a trespass action: trespass is a tort?', you may ask. The theory was that the failure to keep a bargained-for promise was a deceit, and deceit is a tort. So the action for failing to perform an executory contract was, and remained for nearly 300 more years actually, technically, a tortious action for deceit.

One could go into any amount of detail about the development of *assumpsit*. If you wish to read all the detail, then Baker's *An Introduction to English Legal History*, already cited and Simpson's *A History of the Common Law of Contract: The Rise of the Action of Assumpsit*[17] are readily available in libraries. In the meantime, we'll fast-forward a couple of hundred years or so and see what the innovators of the nineteenth century achieved, which was a good deal.

The nineteenth century: How *assumpsit* turned into breach of contract

Historians sometimes speak of 'long' centuries. That is to say, a period of time roughly corresponding to a particular century, but extending some way before and/or after the century proper. For instance, the nineteenth century proper consists of the years 1801 to 1900 inclusive (not 1800 because there was never a year 0 AD, so the first century AD began with 1 AD, the second century with 101 AD and so on), but an historian might write of a 'long nineteenth century' starting in, say, 1779 (French Revolution) and ending in 1914 (when World War I started, changing the world forever). For the lawyer, at any rate the contract lawyer, we might speak of a 'displaced nineteenth century'

---

15 Baker, op. cit., p.279.
16 *Slade v Morley* (1602) 4 Co Rep 92.
17 A.W.B. Simpson, *A History of the Common Law of Contract* (Oxford University Press: Oxford, 1975).

running from 1761 to 1852. The end of the period saw the abolition of the forms of action (the system of having a specific writ with fixed formulae of words for each action) in the Common Law Procedure Act 1852.[18] The beginning saw the publication of Pothier's *Traité des Obligations*. Alternatively, we could speak of a 'short nineteenth century' still ending in 1854 but beginning with 1805 when the first English translation of Pothier appeared; or even one ending in 1854 but beginning in 1790 with the publication of Powell's *Essay on the Law of Contracts and Agreements*.[19] We will feel free to extend over any of these.

Pothier (pronounced *poe-tee-ay*) was a Frenchman and the author of a treatise on obligations. The treatise, forerunner of the modern textbook, is really a creature of the late eighteenth century. Some of the features are familiar in the textbook of today. There is an attempt to define an area of law, such as contracts, to cover the whole of the chosen subject, to dispense with, or at least separate off, specific instances, and to concentrate on general statements. In form, they were inspired very largely by Pothier's *Traité des Obligations*. Even though no English translation appeared until 1805, it should be remembered that an upper-class English boy's education at the time consisted almost wholly of languages, so some jurists, at least, would have been able to enjoy Pothier in the original French (although this should not be overstated: the schools' emphasis was on Latin and Greek).

What is rather different from the modern textbook, however, is that there was almost invariably a special intention running alongside that of making an accurate exposition of the law. Pothier goes to a lot of trouble to demonstrate that the law everywhere is really much the same, and certainly based on the same rationales, and it was all begotten by a Roman sire out of an Aristoteilian-Scholastic dam. Other treatises of the late eighteenth century essentially sought to do this too, and the habit is still noticeable well into the early nineteenth century (see the early editions of Chitty, for instance).

It is generally acknowledged that Pothier's great contribution to classical contract law and theory is the notion of mutual consent; what today we call 'agreement', although it is also inextricably linked with the notion of 'intention to create legal relations', as Simpson points out.[20] This was not as such a feature of the action of *assumpsit* until late in the eighteenth century.[21] *Assumpsit*, as we have seen, involved an action on the case, the allegation being that the defendant had taken the benefit of rights to himself, thus making himself liable

---

18 15 & 16 Vict. c.76.

19 J.J. Powell, *Essay upon the Law of Contracts and Agreements* (London, 1790).

20 Op. cit., pp.263ff.

21 Although it seems established by 1790, when Powell stated the basic elements of contract as 'First, Parties, Secondly, Consent, Thirdly, an Obligation to be constituted or dissolved'. J.J. Powell, *Essay upon the Law of Contracts and Agreements*, London, 1790, p.vii, quoted in Simpson, op. cit., p.266.

(originally only for misfeasance in a public calling) to compensate the plaintiff. The writ included a count for a *quantum meruit*,[22] which is at odds with the modern claim for damages.[23] This was necessary because a claim for a liquidated sum would need to be brought in debt, which entitled the defendant to wage his law. The point is, that *assumpsit* depended on the idea of the defendant taking the benefit of the plaintiff's consideration, whereas classical contract law depends primarily on the notion of a mutual agreement between the parties, supported and made enforceable by consideration or formality.

For the rest, however, what distinguishes truly classical writers on contract from their predecessors is really in their *difference* from Pothier. Pothier saw contract in terms of part of an overarching and unified law of obligations. The classical authors saw contract as a completely distinct notion from other types of obligation. Pothier sought to demonstrate that the law of obligations was essentially universal. The classical writers saw contract law as particular. For Pothier, the question of obligations was as much moral as legal, and the treatise includes a good deal of discussion about moral obligations as distinct from legal ones. Legal obligations were owed to one another, but obligations that the law does not enforce yet the mass of people think ought to be respected, are explained in religious terms: the purely moral aspect of any obligation is owed to God, and we answer for breach of it before the Heavenly Throne, not before an earthly court of law. For the classical writers, the concern was with the law, not with the morality, even if some, notably Sir Frederick Pollock, in his correspondence with Oliver Wendell Holmes Jr, certainly seem to have assumed that there is a morality of promise-keeping at the heart of the legal enforcement of contracts.[24] Finally, while Pothier sought a source in Roman law for each of the doctrines, the classical writers sought no better source than the common law: the English (and American) law of contracts was underived and indigenous. We think there is something in that view. The modern action for breach of contract grew out of *assumpsit*, the rules of which were developed in the common law courts, which were antipathetic to Roman influences, as White explains:

> A general objection arose in the courts of law and throughout the country to the encroachments of the Church of Rome, and connected therewith a general intolerance of the Roman law, which was the law known and

---

22 *Quantum meruit* means 'as much as it is worth'. It is a claim for a reasonable sum for work done and these days in common law jurisdictions is a claim for money in what are called 'restitution' actions. You might like to look up *quantum meruit* and 'restitution' in a law dictionary.

23 See A.M. White, *Outlines of Legal History* (Swan Sonnenschein: London, 1895), p.143ff.

24 Holmes himself, as we shall see in Chapter 3, did not see the performance of contracts as a legal duty at all, and the modern notion of efficient breach seems to suggest that it is not a moral one either, and it may even be, in a sense, *immoral* not to breach in some cases.

administered by the ecclesiastics. A code of laws arose in Chancery distinct from the common law, and based upon the wider jurisprudence of the Roman law.[25]

The myth of the 'ancient constitution', which was such a feature of Victorian intellectual life must, we think, be assumed to have had at least a subliminal influence on the major contract scholars of the early classical era, and would point to just such an aboriginalist view of the doctrines of contract law: what is going on in the courts is not so much *development*, as the ever more refined and accurate discovery of the true law of the English people.

By the middle of the nineteenth century, then, something new and different was beginning to emerge: the beginnings of the truly *classical* text, rooted in a 'scientific' notion of the common law, distinctively different from Pothier and the authors most influenced by him. The content of the law of contract, however, if not the way of writing about it, had in a sense crystallised, as to its basic elements, in a way much influenced by Pothier, through early nineteenth-century texts like Chitty. The basic features were agreement, intention, and consideration, of which only the last really belonged in the old action of *assumpsit*. The distinct action of *assumpsit* was finally abolished, along with the other forms of action, in 1852, but it was really already the carcase of the old action, eaten out from the inside by the new doctrine of breach of contract. What that new idea really was and how it caught on is explained in the next chapter.

Leading cases and the textbook tradition

From the Middle Ages, legal education in England was of two sorts. First, in the two universities, Oxford and Cambridge, the student could learn canon law (the law of the Roman church), later (after the Reformation broke England from the Pope) the civil law, which is to say Roman law, which formed the basis for the canon law and ecclesiastical law of the reformed Church of England. These 'civilians' conducted cases in the ecclesiastical (church, from the Latin *ecclesia*) courts, which covered all wills and inheritance cases, divorces and cases involving clergy. They also practised in the Court of Admiralty, since the law of the sea was based on Roman models. As these practitioners often gained the degree of Doctor of Civil Law (at Oxford) or Doctor of Laws (at Cambridge) (today abbreviated DCL and LLD, respectively) they were referred to as Doctors of the Law or as 'Doctors of the Arches' (because they practised in the church courts, the most important of which was, and is, the Court of Arches) and formed a society near St Paul's churchyard in London called Doctors' Commons, where they practised as the equivalent of barristers

---

25 White, op.cit., pp.21–22.

alongside the Proctors who were the equivalent of what we would now call solicitors. Charles Dickens' character, David Copperfield, works for a while in Doctors' Commons. But the secular jurisdiction of the church courts was removed in 1857, leaving only canon and ecclesiastical law. This led to the doctors throwing in the towel: no new doctors were admitted, the library was sold in 1861 and the buildings were sold in 1865. The last member of Doctors' Commons was Dr T.H. Tristram, who died in 1912. The degrees of DCL and LLD are still bestowed by English universities as a 'higher doctorate' recognising long years of published work, usually after a PhD, but have nothing to do with the civilian jurisdiction in England and confer no rights of audience in any courts.

The other route was to train in the common law as either a barrister or an attorney. The attorneys' place was eventually taken in England by the solicitors, but you can read about all this in a standard book on legal history, if you wish. Barristers-to-be learned their law in the Inns of Court, which began to be established from about 1270 or so in the leafy, even rural, area which then lay between the City of London and Westminster, which latter was then the chief palace of the King and also the seat of the royal courts of law. The Inns of Court, Gray's Inn, Lincoln's Inn, Middle Temple and Inner Temple are still in that area today, although it is now anything but rural and is only leafy in the beautiful and historic gardens of the Inns themselves. In 1882 the chief royal courts joined them in this legal district of London when the Royal Courts of Justice opened in the Strand. This great neo-Gothic building is a little reminiscent of one of the great Victorian railway stations, prompting the actor, playwright and wit, Arthur W. Pinero, to remark *'c'est magnifique, mais ce n'est pas la gare'*.[26]

Education in the Inns of Court was an expensive option, with no scholarships or other arrangements for student funding, such as the 'servitorships' at the universities where a boy could work as a college servant in exchange for lodging and tuition: so the Inns of Court were a preserve of the sons of the gentry and of well-to-do merchants and the like. The education they received was primarily in the form of hearing readings and expositions from statutes, law reports and 'digests' and from reading these things privately, from engaging in mock legal arguments known as moots and from attending the royal courts in Westminster Hall (this building, the oldest part of the British Houses of Parliament is still the original building and can be visited, but the booths around the sides where the different courts were set up have, of course, long gone). Special seats were created in Westminster Hall to allow students to hear what was going on and take notes.

---

26 'It's magnificent, but it isn't the railway station', a play on words on the remark of the French general Bosquet after witnessing the Charge of the Light Brigade at Balaclava in the Crimean War, who is reported to have said *'C'est magnifique, mais ce n'est pas la guerre'* ('it's magnificent, but it isn't war'). (Keble College, Oxford, also claims the dubious honour of its buildings being the subject of this witticism).

The aspect of this education that interests us here is the books that were used, specifically law reports and digests. The earliest surviving law reports are known as the Year Books. No one knows who wrote these reports, which began to appear from the 1280s. It was once thought that there were official reporters, possibly the prothonotaries of the common pleas, but as there are no records of any payments to or appointments of any official reporters, this is no longer believed to be the case. They provided something very important that did not previously exist. The official rolls of the court showed what was formally pleaded and what was decided, but it gave none of the oral argument and reasoning of the serjeants and the judges, in which could be found the actual principles of the common law. The Year Books supplied this; sometimes in a quite lively and informal style that has led to the suggestion, which may well be correct, that they were compiled by students attending to learn and take notes at the courts in Westminster Hall. These reports did not always name the case, or give any of the necessary reference to allow them to be matched up with the official rolls, so they were clearly not official supplements to the formal information of the rolls. Given the lack of author, they were simply designated after the year, by which the cases could be cited, hence 'Year Book'.

The Year Books went on being published until 1535. Other reports came into being during this time, such as Benloe's (reports of the King's Bench from 1440–1627), Benlow's (Common Pleas, 1257–1579), Dyer (common law courts, 1513–1581), some of which were published posthumously and some of which were spuriously attributed to their supposed authors, even including cases decided after the alleged author's death and in one instance including a note of his death! Early sets of reports often included reports of moots and debates held in the Inns of Court as well as of cases decided in the courts. There are various collections of cases made at a later time but including cases from that period, e.g., Eagle & Young's *Collection of Tithe Cases*, covering 1204–1825. But it was the Year Books that began the tradition of law students, in the Inns of Court (and the Inns of Chancery)[27] studying standard written accounts of the decisions of judges, systematically recorded. Indeed, the beginnings of the Year Books coincide with the beginning of the Inns and it

27 These were junior societies of law students and attorneys situated in the legal district around the Inns of Court. They were Clifford's Inn, Clement's Inn, New Inn, Staple Inn, Barnard's Inn, Furnival's Inn, the Strand Inn, Lyon's Inn and Thavie's Inn. These are nowadays effectively defunct and their buildings long since gone, except that the buildings of Barnard's Inn now survive as the home of Gresham College, and Staple Inn as some very quaint office accommodation and the headquarters of the Institute of Actuaries. The gatehouse of Clifford's Inn also survives, tucked between Fleet Street and the old Public Records Office, now the library of King's College, London. Barnard's Inn and Staple Inn were particularly attached to Gray's Inn, which has in recent years revived the custom of a reader being sent from an Inn of Court to its associated Inns of Chancery to give a lecture (called a 'reading'), by establishing an annual public reading at Barnard's Inn, courtesy of Gresham College.

is possible that the reports themselves have no individual authors because they might initially have been the result of collaborative note taking and note sharing among students at the Inns, although Sir John Baker observes that because from about 1350 to about 1450 there appears to be only one basic text, this continuity 'implies some form of organization, with either a single line of reporters or a definite editorial body; but no evidence as to the form of that organization has survived'.[28] Although Lincoln's Inn has the oldest surviving records (the 'Black Books'), this is a weak foundation for claiming to be the oldest Inn. There is ample evidence that Sir Reginald de Gray, Justice of Chester in the 1270s and 1280s had his London house (called an inn in those days – it does not mean 'public house' or hotel in this context) where Gray's Inn stands now, in the 1270s. It is highly likely that he had barristers and students of the law lodging there and forming at least an informal society. Anyway, the newly introduced Year Books, whether organised or ad hoc, perhaps with student involvement, would have been a splendid potential resource for those students to learn from as a supplement to personal attendance at Westminster Hall and they formed the foundation for all future law reporting. What is most important for us is that there was an editorial process at work. There is not a perfect matching with the court rolls and indeed it is not possible by and large to identify a rolls record with a year book report. The cases are selected and the arguments summarised and some cases come to be referred to more than others. The tradition of leading cases is born in this era, to be perfected much later.

From forms to form: The textbook and the transition from eighteenth- to nineteenth-century law writing

The legal world of eighteenth-century England was a world of forms of action, apprenticeship, the 'lawyer as plumber' as Twining would put it,[29] of reports of dubious reliability[30] and of abridgements and digests. Law books tend to be produced either because there is a demand for a particular kind of work, or because the author has a theory and wishes to blaze a trail. It is well understood that law books until the late eighteenth century were intended for the apprentice lawyer, the practitioner and the judge. The forms were law reports, digests of cases, and books of precedent documents. Although law reports and digests still exist, they have only a cosmetic resemblance to their eighteenth-century counterparts. The digests were more like modern casebooks, beloved of students, than *The Digest*, shunned and avoided by today's undergraduate.

28 Baker, op. cit., p.153.
29 W. Twining, *Law in Context* (Clarendon Press: Oxford, 1997), ch.4. We mean that a lot of the literature of the law came in the form of books of pleadings – 'how to' manuals for the practitioner.
30 See later discussion.

Law reports, although outwardly similar to the reports of the nineteenth century and today, were in fact rather different. A law report was not necessarily a faithful account of what was said in a case. We cannot actually say whether any individual report was or was not, since we have no one who can give us an eyewitness account of what happened in court. Certainly, however, many reports essentially consisted of an account of the facts as found, the outcome of the case, and the reporter's opinion as to what the reasoning should have been, dressed up as the judge's actual judgment. The main use they were put to was that of instruction in the Inns of Court and Chancery. This is no doubt why we have two completely inconsistent reports of the judgment in *Stilk v Myrick*.[31] Espinasse's account is now looked on with disfavour, while Campbell's is accepted because Campbell's reasoning appealed more to later judges. Campbell may even have been accurate, but we will never know. One of the present authors recalls, however, once being told of a judge in the nineteenth century who, on being referred by counsel to a report by Espinasse, exclaimed 'I don't want to hear from Espinasse, or any kind of ass!', so perhaps Campbell was regarded as a relatively safe pair of hands.

We have the equivalent of the old precedent books today: *Atkins Court Forms*, *The Encyclopaedia of Forms and Precedents* and Bullen, Leake and Jacob's *Queen's Bench Forms* are examples of this sort of book in modern-day England. But nobody tries to learn the law from them as they do from textbooks and casebooks, and the undergraduate is certainly most unlikely to encounter them.

We saw earlier in this chapter that a distinct tradition arose of the 'treatise' which became the forerunner of the modern textbook. The treatise, as we saw, was a creation of the eighteenth century: Pothier, originally published in the 1750s in France led the way, the earliest native English treatise on contracts is probably that of Powell, called (a little misleadingly in today's language) an *Essay upon the Law of Contracts and Agreements*, which was published in London in 1790. Powell is quite interesting because we see there, perhaps, the appearance of the notion of 'agreement' in the context of the action of assumpsit, when Powell lists the basic elements of a contract as consisting of 'First, Parites, Secondly, Consent, Thirdly, an Obligation to be constituted or dissolved' - there seems to be a bit more there than one usually thinks of as being necessary conditions for an action for assumpsit, at least in earlier times.

By the middle of the 19th century, then, something new and different was beginning to emerge: the beginnings of the truly *classical* text, rooted in a 'scientific' notion of the common law, distinctively different from Pothier and the authors most influenced by him. The content of the law of contract, however, if not the way of writing about it, had in a sense crystallized, as to

31 (1809) 6 Esp. 129, 170 ER 851; 2 Camp. 317, 170 ER 1168.

Figure 2.1 The Royal Courts of Justice, London: 'C'est magnifique, Mais ce n'est pas
         la gare'.

This photograph is licensed under the Creative Commons Licence.

its basic elements, in a way much influenced by Pothier, through early 19th
century texts like Chitty. The basic features were agreement, intention, and
consideration, of which only the last really belonged in the old action of
assumpsit.

   Three publishing events centuries after the Year Book era can be considered
as cementing and perfecting the idea of the leading case and of establishing
the modern idea of the law textbook. First, the consignment to history of most
of the named series of reports (those series named after either their real
reporter or after a well-known lawyer whose name would give weight to the
reports, even if he were already dead before they were published; Baker gives
some examples of this). They were replaced in England by the establishment
law reports, published by the Incorporated Council of Law Reporting for
England and Wales. The reduction of many series to one official set of reports
for the superior courts narrowed the scope of cases likely to get reported and
therefore referred to in the courts.

The second was the publication of Langdell's *Selection of Cases in the Law of Contract* in 1871. Christopher Columbus Langdell was named the first Dean of Harvard Law School in 1870. He had admired the Oxford system of teaching through tutorials in which the tutor would listen to the student's essay on a topic set at the previous tutorial and then quiz him on it, engaging in a Socratic dialogue with the student for an hour or so. Langdell had nothing like the necessary number of staff to achieve this approach at Harvard. Instead, he devised a new method of engaging in depth with students that would work with a roomful: the case class. This way, a Socratic exchange could take place between tutor and one student, but the rest of the students in the room could have the benefit of listening in on it. When Langdell took over at Harvard, the law library was contained in one room, looked after by the janitor of Dane Hall. This would clearly be inadequate to provide dozens of law students each with a copy of the same report of the same case to study and write a brief on at the same time for the same class. A book was needed that students could buy that contained all the necessary cases. And this was it. The book contained complete reprints of all the cases Langdell wished to use, divided into three broadly defined parts with little if any subdivision and no commentary. This was not to be a textbook, but a book containing the 'leading cases' on the law of contract.

The third was not so much a publishing event as a succession of publications from about the 1870s: the publication of systematic, scientific and brief (350 pages or so) textbooks of contract law aimed at the law student and confined to a number of general principles of substantive contract doctrine (rather than lengthy disquisitions on formalities and procedures and detailed accounts of the jurisprudence of various different types of contract by subject matter). The outstanding examples of such texts are Pollock (1876) and Anson (1878). Anson (now in its 29th edition) is still in use in some English law schools today (including Lancaster). Pollock not only had multiple English editions but three American editions before being replaced by home-grown treatises. Textbooks of this length must necessarily ignore the overwhelming majority of reported cases and focus on a relatively few that are considered by the textbook author in question to be especially exemplary and authoritative on the point in question: in short, the leading cases. The leading cases approach made the modern law text possible. The modern law text, in turn, cemented the tradition of leading cases. Each also made possible the perfection, if that is the right word, of classical contract, which is the subject of the first part of the next chapter.

Suggested further reading

J.H. Baker, *An Introduction to Legal History*, 2nd edn (Butterworths: London, 1979).

C.H.W. Johns, *The Oldest Code of Laws in the World: The Code of Laws Promulgated by Hammurabi, King of Babylon B.C. 2285–2242* (T. & T. Clark: Edinburgh, 1903). This is very dated and the scholarship has been superseded, but it is a good source for the text of the Code.

H.W.F. Saggs, *The Greatness that was Babylon* 2nd edn (Sidgwick & Jackson: London, 1988) [reprinted as *The Babylonians* (Folio: London, 1999)]

A.W.B. Simpson, *A History of the Common Law of Contract* (Oxford University Press: Oxford, 1975).

3 Classical and neo-classical contract

- The rise of the classical general theory of contracts
- The will theory of contract and contract as promise
- The birth of 'realism' and neo-classical contract
- The 'death of contract'

The rise of the classical general theory of contracts

We saw in Chapter 2 how actions for breach of contract in the common law evolved from the actions of debt and *assumpsit* (and also, in a way, from *detinue* and from covenant). In this chapter, we will be looking at not so much the development of law in the courts by judges and by courtroom lawyers (and, to be fair, contract draughtsmen in law offices), but rather the development by academic jurists of what we call the 'classical general theory of contracts' in England and the US.

In Chapter 2, we discussed the textbook tradition and you will have seen how the modern textbook came about, built on the idea of leading cases and on the idea, essential to the textbook project and, indeed, the whole approach of studying the law as an academic discipline, that the law in any given area – in this case, contracts – can be reduced to a relatively small number of governing principles. By the middle of the nineteenth century, then, something new and different was beginning to emerge in response to these ideas and to meet these needs: the beginnings of the truly *classical* text, rooted in a 'scientific' notion of the common law, distinctively different from Pothier and the authors most influenced by him. The content of the law of contract, however, if not the way of writing about it, had in a sense crystallised, as to its basic elements, in a way much influenced by Pothier, through early nineteenth-century texts such as Chitty. The basic features were agreement, intention, and consideration, of which only the last really belonged in the old action of *assumpsit*.

Beginnings

According to Gilmore, the general theory of contract was the invention of Langdell, and appears in his *Selection of Cases on Contracts*.[1] This seems a little hard to credit. It is far from clear how a book consisting wholly of reprints of cases, arranged into only three chapters ('Mutual consent', 'Consideration' and 'Conditional contracts') with only limited subdivision (none at all in the first chapter, some 163 pages in length) with no commentary at all by the 'editor', who has not even selected particular sections of judgments, but simply reproduces each report in full, can be said to expound a theory at all, let alone so refined and elegant a thing as 'classical contract theory'. The introduction to the book concerns itself only with the pedagogical purpose of the work, and the division of the subject is less sophisticated than Addison's, and a long way from the modernity of Anson (1879). Realistically, we cannot precisely date the birth of 'the law of contract', as Gilmore purports to do; but it seems first to have appeared (or begun to emerge) in England during the middle decades of the nineteenth century. Works such as Addison's *Treatise on the Law of Contracts*,[2] represented a halfway house between the old-fashioned type of treatise or digest and the modern textbook. Developing through works such as Pollock's *Principles of Contract at Law and Equity* (1876)[3] and Leake's *The Elements of the Law of Contracts* (1878),[4] the classical general theory of contract (and with it contract textbooks) finally reached what may fairly be described as a degree of maturity in Anson.[5] From then on, development of the theory, and the growth of its influence on lawyers and the courts, was rapid.

Although intellectual pressure for the systematisation of the common law can be dated at least to Austin,[6] the modern conception of contract law as a systematic set of principles derived from case law might fairly be attributed to this succession of English writers, and to the Americans who followed them and, ultimately, played a leading rôle in spreading the gospel. It is true that in 1837 Justice Joseph Story in his report to the Governor of Massachusetts on the codification of the common law claimed that the law on commercial

---

1 C.C. Langdell, *Selection of Cases on Contracts* (Little, Brown & Co.: Boston, MA, 1871).

2 C.G. Addison, Treatise on the Law of Contracts and Parties to Actions Ex Contractu (W. Benning & Co.: London, 1847).

3 Sir F. Pollock, *Principles of Contract at Law and Equity* (Stevens & Sons: London, 1876).

4 S.M. Leake, *The Elements of the Law of Contracts* (London, 1878). (According to the British Library catalogue, another edition exists under the title *An Elementary Digest of the Law of Contracts*, presumably of an earlier date (as the wording of the title tends to suggest), which is presumably the 'Leake' quoted from in Langdell, as to which see later.)

5 Sir W. Anson, *Principles of the English Law of Contract* (Clarendon Press: Oxford, 1879).

6 Whose own contribution, although much less sophisticated in its taxonomy than that of later writers, should not be minimised: the division into voluntarily assumed and non-voluntary liability was a fair step for the time. It is true, though, that Pollock had little time for him: 'The truth is that his law is thoroughly amateurish – his Roman law almost worse than his English – and this is why he has a reputation among half-educated publicists' (5 July 1899, Pollock-Holmes Letters, vol. I, p.94).

contracts had 'attained . . . scientific precision' and that 'the general principles which define and regulate them . . . are now capable of being put in a regular order, and announced in determinate propositions in the text of a code',[7] but he did not actually propose anything like the scheme we would expect today in a textbook on contract, that is to say 'Agreement', 'Intention to create legal relations', 'Consideration' and so on, but instead a code of commercial contracts divided into separate titles dealing successively with agency, bailments, guaranty, suretyship, bills of exchange, insurance, etc. So it was not particularly 'general' in reality. This approach was carried through in the books he wrote as Dane Professor at Harvard: separate *Commentaries* on agency (1839), partnership (1841), bills of exchange (1843), promissory notes (1845) and so on.

Contrariwise, only some 30 years later Langdell, perhaps influenced by English authors such as Leake whose work he had read, is thought to have had in mind very much the sort of general principles we recognise today as making up the law of contract. Sutherland, in his book *The Law at Harvard*, thought that the reason William Eliot, the President of Harvard College, appointed Langdell as Dane Professor of Law was 'Eliot's and Langdell's common intellectual commitment to the scientism of the day'.[8] In a speech to the Harvard Law School Association in 1886, Langdell said that it was 'essential to establish . . . that law is a *science*'[9] (our emphasis); and Langdell's work as a teacher was aimed at making it just that: teaching his students that what we might characterise as 'the laws of contract law' existed and were discoverable from the printed reports of cases.[10] Langdell wrote in the preface to his casebook that:

> Law, considered as a science, consists of certain principles or doctrines . . . Moreover the number of fundamental legal doctrines is much less than is commonly supposed; the many different guises in which the same doctrine is constantly making its appearance . . . being the cause of much misapprehension.

7 J. Story, *Report on the Codification of the Common Law* (1837), quoted in G. Gilmore, *The Death of Contract* (Ohio State University Press: Columbus, OH, 1974), p.10.

8 A.E. Sutherland, *The Law at Harvard* (Belknap Press: Cambridge, MA, 1967), p.166.

9 Sutherland, op. cit., p.175. It is interesting to note that American universities to this day offer JSD or SJD (Doctor of Juridical *Science*) degree programmes for those intending an academic career, where intending law academics in England pursue research for a PhD as in other disciplines.

10 Sutherland further observes (loc. cit.) that: 'In 1870 the word "science" carried connotations quite different from its eighteenth century meaning . . . no longer widely used to describe any organized body of knowledge. . .' but that Langdell's 'gospel was the application of the method of the natural sciences to the science of society. To him the proper study of the law, like the study of chemistry, physics, zoology, and botany, consisted in the careful observation and recording of many specific instances, and then from these instances derivation of *general conclusions that the qualities of the phenomena or specimens observed would hold constant for other instances of the same classes*' (p.176; emphasis added).

In other words, the law in any given field can be expressed in a fairly limited number of doctrines: in the case of contract law, these are agreement, consideration, form, and so on, that we recognise today in our textbooks and our lecture courses.

Addison, too, had written of law as a science. In the March 1847 preface (his work has two prefaces, one dated 'June 12th 1845' and the other dated 'March 1847', in the year of publication), he wrote that: '[S]ome attempt has been made to recommence the teaching of the law as a science, in localities where it has long been practised only as an art.'[11] Unlike his predecessors, Addison evidently thought it possible to deal with a considerable part of the law of contracts in general terms. It may be worthwhile to consider Addison's arrangement. It is notable that, of a book consisting of some 886 pages (plus index, tables, etc.), some 428 pages are devoted to dealing with general propositions. The first edition of Anson, which deals, as do most modern contract texts, solely with contract as a general theory, totals only some 338 pages. The main difference is that in the general part of Addison, the order in which matters are dealt with, the emphasis put on specialties, the relative length of treatment of different aspects of contract law, and so on, are quite different from what we would expect to see today. Much of modern contract theory *is there* – offer, mirror-image acceptance, consideration, privity and so forth – but it is presented in a fashion that is alien to contemporary lawyers.

By 1879, however, we have in Anson the modern contract textbook. If we substitute 'offer' for 'proposal' and 'illegality' for 'legality of object' we have a list of contents that we should not be surprised to see in the front of a brand-new contract text. As for Langdell, in 1872 he produced *Cases on Sales*, and in 1880 he added to his contracts casebook a 'Summary of the Law of Contracts'. Besides these, he seems not to have published a great deal more and the classical general theory of contract was left for others, notably Anson, Holmes, Pollock, Williston and Ames, to develop.

Williston perhaps shed some light on how it was that, in the last decades of the nineteenth century, a whole new theory of contract should take root so quickly and with so little resistance, when he wrote that:

> There had been little theoretical discussion prior to the Commentaries of Blackstone of any branches of private law other than those relating to real property and to crimes. It was comparatively easy, therefore, to adopt a new theory of contract, since any inconsistency with earlier notions was not obvious enough to be disturbing. [12]

---

11 Addison, loc. cit.
12 S. Williston, 'Freedom of Contract' (1921) 6 *Cornell LQ* 365, reproduced in Association of American Law Schools, *Selected Readings on the Law of Contracts* (Macmillan: New York, 1931), pp.100, 103.

Holmes

BIO NOTE

Oliver Wendell Holmes Jr was born in Boston, Massachusetts, on 8 March 1841, the son of Oliver Wendell Holmes Sr, who was a physician and also a distinguished 'man of letters' and of Amelia Lee Jackson, a noted campaigner for the abolition of slavery. He followed in his father's footsteps in studying at Harvard and served (seeing a lot of action) in the Massachusetts militia in the American Civil War.

Following the war, he returned to Harvard, this time to the Law School, under his father's influence. He was admitted to the bar in 1866 and in due course went into practice in a small firm in Boston. In 1872 he married a childhood friend, Fanny Bowditch Dixwell. They had no children of their own but adopted a daughter, Dorothy.

In autumn 1882 Holmes became a professor at Harvard Law School, but in December of the same year accepted a seat on the Massachusetts Supreme Court, resigning from Harvard without notice – which did not go down well! In 1899 he became Chief Justice of the Massachusetts Supreme Court; then in 1902, he was appointed an Associate Justice of the United States Supreme Court by President Theodore Roosevelt. He served in this capacity until 1932. Fanny died in 1929. Holmes died on 6 March 1935.

In 1881 Oliver Wendell Holmes Jr published *The Common Law*,[13] still today perhaps the most famous law book in the common law world after Blackstone's *Commentaries*, although probably few people read it today. Holmes' great contribution to Anglo-American legal theory in general is commonly said to be the fathering of 'realism', set against 'formalism' in the great legal contest of the twentieth century. His contributions to contract theory in particular were, first, the idea that there is no duty to perform and, second, the 'bargain theory of consideration'. Gilmore also credits him ('and his successors') with the objective test of agreement.[14]

Holmes' actual contribution to realism will be discussed further later, as it seems far from obvious that Holmes could be considered a realist at all – it is, for instance, unclear where he could have fitted in to Llewellyn's sample of

---

13 O.W. Holmes Jr, *The Common Law*, M. deWolfe Howe edn (Macmillan: London, 1968).
14 Gilmore, op. cit., at pp.35ff.

realists,[15] since Holmes was not a 'young teacher of law', not 'a rule sceptic', made no case at all for 'empirical'[16] research, and unlike practically all of those listed by Llewellyn, was a practitioner and judge, as well as a teacher.[17] Moreover, he was, through-and-through a Harvard man, while the realist movement was very much a creature of Columbia and Yale, and very largely the product of curriculum review and the tensions between the traditional American view of the professional law school and the 'social sciences' or 'academic' views of Llewellyn's 'younger teachers of law'.[18] We could go further. In his critique of Holmes, Atiyah cites criticisms of Holmes by Hart and Fuller 'that Holmes's theory focuses too much on the judicial and remedial aspects of the law. Law exists in the outside world, not merely in the courts',[19] yet surely that is precisely the opposite of calling him of being a realist, since realism very much takes account of the wider context of law.

It is quite hard at this at this distance in time to assess Holmes' contribution to contract theory as such. In *The Common Law* only three of 11 'lectures' deal with contracts, and one of those is very much an essay in legal history, concentrating on methods of proof in mediaeval times.

The lack of a duty to perform

Holmes' chief argument (and what we might call the first element of the theory) has been described as a paradox: that there is no obligation to perform, only a conditional obligation to pay damages for non-performance, which can be avoided by actually performing. As Holmes put it:

> The only universal consequence of a legally binding promise is, that the law makes the promisor pay damages if the promised event does not come

---

15 See K. Llewellyn, 'Some Realism about Realism' (1931) 44 *Harvard LR* 1222, p.1226 n.18, cited in W. Twining, *Karl Llewellyn and the Realist Movement* (Weidenfeld & Nicholson: London, 1973), pp.75ff. Twining reproduces the list at p.76.

16 The reason for the quotation marks around 'empirical' should become apparent later, in the discussion of the realists proper.

17 The only practitioners listed by Llewellyn were Frank and Klaus. The appointment of non-practitioners to law school posts in America was an innovation of Langdell's at Harvard, and treated with some suspicion for a long time afterwards (see, generally, Sutherland, op. cit.).

18 See Twining, op. cit., cc.3 and 4. In England, university law schools have traditionally been purely academic, with the professional training aspect being left to the College of Law (now, absurdly, called the 'University of Law') for intending solicitors and the Inns of Court School of Law for intending barristers, plus a period of supervised professional experience in a law office or barristers' chambers. Many university law schools in England do now undertake professional training, but it is kept quite separate from the academic preparation of the law degree or law conversion course, which must be completed before professional studies are begun.

19 Sir P.S. Atiyah, *Essays on Contract* (Clarendon Press: Oxford, 1986), p.60.

to pass. In every case it leaves him free from interference until the time for fulfilment has gone by, and therefore free to break his contract if he chooses.[20]

At first blush a rather *unreal* position for a 'realist', if such Holmes was, as Pollock pointed out:

> A man who bespeaks a coat of his tailor will scarcely be persuaded that he is only betting with the tailor that such a coat will not be made and delivered within a certain time. What he wants and means to have is the coat, not an insurance against not having a coat.[21]

Although (perhaps in response to this criticism from Pollock) Holmes concedes that '[I]t is true that, when people make contracts, they usually contemplate the performance rather than the breach.'[22] Atiyah thinks that Holmes actually 'greatly understated one of the strongest arguments for his own theory' when making this last statement quoted, on the grounds that '[T]his is, in truth, very far from being a universal consequence of a legally binding promise – the law only makes the promisor pay damages when the promisee has suffered what the law characterizes as a loss.'[23] Atiyah, however, seems to forget what Holmes perhaps did not forget: that where no measurable loss can be proved (we say *proved* rather than suffered, because that is the real issue when a court inquires into the quantum of damages) the courts will award nominal damages, so that the award of damages *can* be regarded as a 'universal consequence'. What is not taken account of in Holmes' theory is the element of accident in damages becoming the primary remedy. An award of damages was the remedy in an action of *assumpsit*. The remedy, at common law, in an action of covenant was an order akin to specific performance. *Assumpsit* simply became the principal, and eventually only, action for breach of contract, so that damages became the common law remedy for breach of a contract, with a decree of specific performance available only in equity in cases where damages would be an inadequate remedy (including many cases where there is no provable financial loss).[24] Holmes' argument seems to be, however, that the availability

---

20 Holmes, op. cit., p.236.
21 Sir F.W. Pollock, *Principles of Contract*, 3rd edn, (1881), p.xix, cited in Atiyah, n.19, p.60. It must be probable that some such example as this was given in a letter from Pollock to Holmes, but I am unable to locate such a letter in the published correspondence – and the earliest reference I can find to this criticism of Holmes in the correspondence is in Holmes' letter to Pollock of 25 March 1883 (M. deWolfe Howe (Ed.), *The Pollock-Holmes Letters, Correspondence of Sir Frederick Pollock and Mr Justice Holmes 1874–1932* (Cambridge University Press: Cambridge, 1942), vol. 1, pp.19–21).
22 Holmes, n.31, p.237.
23 Atiyah, n.19, p.62.
24 See, generally, R. Austen-Baker, 'Difficulties with Damages as a Ground for Specific Performance' (1999) 10 *KCLJ* 1.

only of damages at common law is some sort of article of faith of the common law, which does not seem to accord with what we know of the history of 'contract' actions in *assumpsit* and covenant.

A further argument against this theory of Holmes' is that a party to a contract has an action on the case against a third party who induces the other party to the contract to breach it. If the common law does not recognise a duty to perform, only a conditional obligation to pay damages, avoidable by performing the contract in accordance with its terms, then there could be no loss for which to sue the third party. Yet another good argument is that pointed up by McGovney, that the availability of specific performance and injunctions leads to the conclusion that a promisor does not really have a choice of alternative performances – as stipulated, or else paying damages.[25]

The bargain theory of consideration

'The root of the whole matter [of consideration] is the relation of reciprocal conventional inducement, each for the other, between consideration and promise.'[26] The bargain theory of consideration, in particular, was immensely influential in American contract theory. As to England, Atiyah concedes that Pollock found it attractive and 'almost adopted' it, and that it was 'once approved in the House of Lords'.[27] The case in which the theory was 'once approved in the House of Lords' was *Dunlop Pneumatic Tyre Co v Selfridge*,[28] yet Atiyah asserts that it 'never took firm root in England'.[29] Atiyah does not justify his assertion with any authority to the effect that *Dunlop* is not followed, or even explain what it is he thinks England has had instead. It seems arguable that the various ways of describing consideration really all amount to the same thing – consideration is whatever is given for a promise, as long as it is so treated by the parties. Whether one describes this as 'a detriment suffered by one party or benefit gained by the other party' or as 'the price of the other party's promise' really does not seem to be important. The requirement that consideration 'move' from the claimant clearly demonstrates that it is viewed, in effect, as the price paid for the defendant's promise. At least, that is how the courts put it, whether or not, in reality, it is mere form or anything else one cares to call it. Indeed, we can go a little further than this: the bargain theory's language of the 'price' for a promise, rather than 'benefit' and 'detriment' is really no more than a slightly more realistic way of putting it. We can say this because many things have been held to be good consideration without there being any real benefit or detriment: marriage as consideration,

25 D.O. McGovney, 'Irrevocable Offers' (1914) 27 *Harvard LR* 644.
26 Holmes, op.cit., p.230.
27 Atiyah, op. cit., n.19, p.69.
28 [1915] A.C. 847.
29 Loc. cit., n.19.

for instance. Another classic instance in the English courts is *Chappell & Co. Ltd v Nestlé Co Ltd*,[30] another House of Lords case which seems to affirm the bargain theory.[31]

Anyway, it is clear from the writings of Williston and from the Restatement of Contracts that the bargain theory of consideration certainly took root in America, as these sections of the Restatement of Contracts illustrate:

> *Section 12.* A unilateral contract is one in which no promisor receives a promise as consideration. A bilateral contract is one in which there are mutual promises between two parties to the contract; each party being both a promisor and a promisee.

> *Section 24.* An offer is a promise which is in its terms conditional upon an act, forbearance or counterpromise being *given in exchange* for the promise or its performance. (emphasis added)

Although these sections deal with offer and acceptance, nevertheless this is the bargain theory in quasi-legislative form. It is to be doubted whether Holmes himself thought that this was a new idea, let alone whether it actually was. We ought to be reluctant, perhaps, to cite such a rocky case as *Stilk v Myrick*,[32] but the fact remains that the idea of a promise as the price of a counter-promise hardly can be called a late nineteenth-century novelty.

---

30 [1960] A.C. 87.
31 In this case, the plaintiffs were owners of the rights to a musical piece rejoicing in the title *Rockin' Shoes*, which was included on a record that the defendant confectionery manufacturers offered to the public for the sum of 1s/6d provided they also sent three wrappers from the defendant's milk chocolate bars. Now, under section 8 of the Copyright Act 1956 a person could sell recordings of musical works belonging to another provided they (a) gave prior notice to the copyright owner and (b) paid the copyright owner 6 1/4 per cent of the retail price. The defendant gave due notice to the plaintiffs and specified the retail price as 1s/6d. The plaintiffs sought an injunction to restrain Nestlé on the grounds that the retail price was not 1s/6d but 1s/6d and three wrappers. The House of Lords held by a majority of three to two (Viscount Simonds and Lord Keith of Avonholm dissenting) that the wrappers were not simply another condition of the contract but were part of the consideration, and therefore of the retail price. This case is a good illustration of the difficulty, sometimes, of distinguishing between general conditions of the contract and conditions forming part of the consideration, but we use it here as illustrating the notion of equating consideration with the 'price' of the defendant's promise.
32 (1809) 2 Camp. 317; 6 Esp. 129. The two reports of this case are notoriously at odds with one another. Campbell's report based the decision on what we would today consider to be a classical understanding of consideration, whereas Espinasse had the matter decided on the basis of public policy on seamen's wages. Campbell's report is usually preferred, and Espinasse was regarded even in the early 19th century as somewhat unreliable. It might easily be the case that the judge gave both grounds, much as a great many modern judges give alternative grounds, and each reporter reported the version he judged to be the real *ratio* of the decision.

The objective test of agreement

The argument for Holmes, having invented the objective test of agreement, or even joint authorship of it, seems weakest of all. Gilmore argues at some length, excoriating Holmes and unspecified successors for inventing a rule that did not represent the practice of the courts, who were all busily and happily applying a subjective test. He supports his argument with a discussion of the 'objectification' of *Raffles v Wichelhaus*,[33] and, like so many others seems to confuse the use of the term *consensus ad idem* (Latin for 'agreement to the [same] thing', which played an important part in Pothier's idea of contractual obligation, and came into the consciousness of English lawyers through his *Traité des Obligations*) with the subjective test of the 'meeting of minds'. This suggestion can be dealt with very simply and briefly: if Holmes and his successors thought all this up in America from the 1880s onwards, how did the English judge Blackburn J get hold of it in 1871 so as to assert the primacy of the objective approach in *Smith v Hughes*?[34] As to *consensus ad idem*, this means no more than agreement on the issue or subject matter. Whether there is a *consensus* in this sense is perfectly capable of being judged either subjectively or objectively: use of the phrase says nothing about which approach a judge is taking.

Summarising, it seems that Holmes' contribution is probably not all it has been said to be. The 'no duty to perform' idea was straightaway seen to be paradoxical and to fail to fit either with the reality of expectations (i.e., that people expect performance), the fact that it was a matter chiefly of historical accident that *assumpsit* rather than *covenant* carried contract doctrine forward, or the fact that a party to a contract has an action on the case against a stranger for inducing breach of contract, not to mention frequent judicial pronouncements on the 'duty' of contracting parties to perform their contracts. As an idea, it never affected the law in the courts. The 'bargain theory' looks like it was nothing new, nor particularly distinctive: at any rate, whether one looks at something from the point of view of detrimental reliance, or promise as price of counter-promise, hardly seems to matter. As to 'objectification', more need hardly be said. His extraordinary openness about judicial practice, however, certainly fed into the realist debate of the 1920s and 1930s.

The mature theory in America

Samuel Williston, Professor of Law at Harvard, produced his own casebook in 1894 and his monumental *Treatise on the Law of Contracts* in 1920 (this first edition was in four volumes; by the third edition it had grown to 16 volumes). Williston was a more obviously scholarly figure than Langdell, and he

---

33 (1864) 2 H. & C. 906; 159 ER. 375.
34 (1871) L.R. 6 QB 597.

BIO NOTE

Samuel Williston was born in Cambridge, Massachusetts in 1861. He took his AB at Harvard College in 1882, and his AM and LLB in 1888. He practised law in Boston and Cambridge between 1889 and 1895. In 1890 he became Assistant Professor of Law at Harvard (part-timers currently practising were common at that time on American law school faculties), became a full professor in 1895, Weld Professor in 1903 and Dane Professor in 1919.

---

published extensively. Apart from the works mentioned already, he was author or editor of works on the *Law of Sales* (1909), *Cases on Sales* (1894), *Cases on Bankruptcy* (1902), the eighth edition of *Parsons on Contracts*, and *Stephen on Pleading* (1895), as well as numerous journal articles. Williston had a powerfully analytical mind and was determined to show that the common law was made up of quite a limited number of different concepts. For example, he noted that the language used by the common law judges to discuss contractual agreement was all about subjective intentions – i.e., what each of the parties really meant, in his own mind – but the same judges only used *objective* criteria to decide what was in the parties' minds. In other words, since the law looked to the external (objective) facts as conclusive evidence of internal (subjective) intention, which could not generally be rebutted by any evidence whatever, it was more accurate to say that the test was objective.

Williston argued in an article called 'Freedom of Contract'[35] that the idea of individual freedom as it was viewed in the late eighteenth and the early and middle nineteenth centuries (exemplified by John Stuart Mill) was so absolute that the individual could not be held to have limited his freedom of action by agreement with another unless he gave his inward, mental assent. This led to the use of subjective language when talking about agreement. The increasing *objectivism* of the late nineteenth and early twentieth centuries was really an attempt to return to a traditional rule of objectivity in the common law, and to the dominant position of consideration and reliance in the old action of *assumpsit*.

After this period, much of Williston's time seems to have been spent on the Restatement, the Uniform Sales Act and his treatise, and defending his definitions in the pages of the law reviews. It is also important to note that

---

35   S. Williston, 'Freedom of Contract' (1921) 6 *Cornell LQ* 365.

long before Williston published his treatise, he was annotating the *third* American edition of Pollock (1906), so although Williston was an arch-classicist, he cannot be held responsible for American law students being exposed for the first time to classical contract treatises. It is quite clear that Williston's view of contracts was not wholly his own invention, but highly influenced by earlier English writers. So, we can say that the classical general theory of contracts was developed by academic writers from both England and the United States, influencing one another. It is also fair to say that the approach adopted by these writers – who greatly influenced the future lawyers and future judges whom they taught in the universities – was very narrow and formalistic, and you can see this in the logical contortions the judges go through in many of the great classic cases on contracts, as they try to make their practical decisions fit into the theoretical scheme.

The will theory of contract and contract as promise

We need to say something somewhere about 'contract theory' and what we mean by the phrase, to avoid any confusion. Since this is also a good place to mention one particular theory, 'the will theory', it also looks like a good place to define our terms. There are two basic sorts of theory of contract, which we can call 'general theories' and 'meta-theories'. What we mean by general theories of contract is the idea that we can state a set of rules that govern contracts in general (rather than just a huge morass of different types of contract all governed by their own rules). Such rules we group into areas with names such as 'agreement', 'consideration', 'terms', 'breach', 'frustration' and so on. The classical contract theory we have been talking about in this chapter up to now is a general theory. So is the neo-classicalism we are going to look at shortly. What we shall call 'meta-theories'[36] are ones that rather than trying to set out a framework of principles we say judges use in deciding contract disputes, instead try to explain why the rules are as they are. So, the general theories of contract try to explain *what* the rules are, while the meta-theories try to explain *why* the rules are as they are or even why we have contracts at all and what they really mean. Meta-theories of contract fall into three basic groups:

- promissory theories
- reliance theories
- transfer theories.

Promissory theories basically state that the reason we enforce contracts is because they are promises and because human society thinks promises *ought*

---

36 *Meta* is Greek for 'beyond' or 'above'.

to be kept, as a sort of moral requirement.[37] Reliance theories claim that we enforce contracts because they contain promises that the other person has *relied on* and it would be wrong to let A go back on his word if by giving his word he caused B to change his position (e.g., to buy something from A instead of getting it from C or D) – so the purpose of enforceable contracts is to protect B from harm if he relies on A's promise and A lets him down. Transfer theories are more difficult to understand. They work on the basis that there is a right to performance that, in a manner of speaking, sits out there *in potentia*, as a thing in itself. The right to performance is not created by the contract, but is *transferred* from A to B by the contract.

The classical general theory of contracts is said to be based on the will theory of contracts.[38] This states that the parties to a contract are bound by their promises to each other because each made an act of his own free will to enter into the contract, thus limiting by their own decision their ability to make choices in the future (e.g., if A decides to accept B's offer to buy A's house, then A has, by his own free will, given up the freedom to sell the house to C and B has, by his own free will, committed to handing over a certain amount of money he could have used for something else to A in exchange for his house). It could be suggested that what distinguishes 'neo-classical' contract theory (if you believe in such a thing!) from classical contract theory is that in neo-classical theory, reliance is seen as more important than promise as a motivation for enforcing contracts. By way of contrast, it could be argued that with neo-classical theory, the philosophical motivation for enforcement is simply less important altogether and the more flexible approaches judges appear to take in more recent decades is down to pragmatism taking the place of dogmatic belief in free will. (This difference is important, by the way: if you place free will on a pedestal then you make it more likely that an agreement will be held unenforceable or void because of one party acting under a mistaken belief, for example.) Yet again, we could say that the distinction between promissory and reliance theories is artificial because it could be argued that we enforce contracts because promise keeping is right and promise breaking is wrong, but that keeping is right and breaking is wrong because promises have a habit of being relied on.

---

37 See, e.g., C. Fried, *Contract as Promise* (Harvard University Press: Cambridge, MA, 1981). The reasons for promise keeping being a moral fundamental may be related to the necessities of human cooperation and inter-reliance, without necessarily having a divine source or sanction, though this latter is of course a possible source of moral imperatives.

38 We have seen earlier (p. 48) and will see again (p. 63) that this is quite a doubtful proposition: Williston, who is seen as one of the great architects of classical theory, dismissed assent (i.e., the will of the parties) as the basis of contractual enforceability, because the important thing was outward appearances, not inward state of mind (assent) and the existence of apparent agreement supported by the required consideration or formality was what mattered. In other words, the shapers of the classical theory did not really care about the meta-theoretical basis for enforcement, so classical contract cannot be said to be based on any meta-theoretical justifications.

Legal realism and the rise of 'neo-classical' contract

Perhaps the single great feature of the middle part of the twentieth century in American contract theory is the rise of legal realism, and particularly the towering figures of Arthur Corbin and Karl Llewellyn. However, it is not always easy to pin down what legal realism *is*, or who may fairly be called a legal realist. Three important points must be borne in mind:

- legal realism is law-wide, not just concerned with contract
- legal realism has been tied very strongly to debates about law teaching, rather than being solely a theoretical concern of researchers
- legal realism's proponents were, in the main, centred in a very few institutions.

Professor William Twining describes what Llewellyn (at least) meant by a legal realist:

> A realist is one who, no matter what his ideological or philosophical views, believes that it is important regularly to focus attention on the law in action at any given time and to try to describe as honestly and clearly as possible what is to be seen.[39]

Llewellyn himself made a list of nine assumptions, he called 'points of departure' that realists shared with each other.[40] But we can boil the essentials of legal realism down to five points:

1. 'Rule scepticism': a disbelief in the proposition that rules that anyone may know actually decide cases.
2. 'Fact scepticism': the belief that the judge or jury may make findings of facts that are unpredictable or even contrary to evidence to back up the outcome they want to reach.
3. 'Opinion scepticism': the belief that what judges do and why they do it is at times quite a different thing from what they *say* they do.
4. Following from (3) the belief that it is necessary to look primarily at the *effects* of court decisions rather than at the words of the judgments themselves.
5. 'Empirical' research as a means of ascertaining these effects.

Law professors had argued for most of these things before, although not necessarily as a bundle. What was new in realism was the belief in the importance of 'empirical' work.

---

39 W. Twining, *Karl Llewellyn and the Realist Movement* (Weidenfeld & Nicholson: London, 1973), p.74.
40 For the full text, see Llewellyn, op. cit., at pp.1236–1238.

We do not have the space in this book for a detailed discussion of what 'empirical' research might mean in the legal field. Some would argue that it means 'quantitative' work – counting things. An example of this was William Underhill Moore at Yale, 'sitting on a camp stool in Bermuda shorts in the streets of New Haven solemnly counting cars'[41] in an attempt to judge 'the noneffect on the parking practices of New Haveners of a change in the official regulations which he had arranged to keep carefully from coming to the knowledge of any trafficker'.[42] It might also mean 'counting cases': one looks at a large number of cases with related factual scenarios and then counts up the number of times the decision went one way or another in order to try to construct a hypothesis as to what the rules might be in a similar way to a scientist. For example, rather than take judges' word for it that they decide each child custody case on the basis of a checklist of things affecting the child's best interests, one might want to see how often the father ever gets custody. Are there any factual findings that link those cases together? You might find that in the courts of one jurisdiction the father only actually gets custody against the mother's wishes in cases where the mother's behaviour is so bad that if a public authority applied for an order to take the child into their care, the court would grant such an order. That would be an example of empirical study (and also of rule scepticism and of opinion scepticism).

Legal realists also did conventional library-based work (looking at law reports to see what they say, which is 'empirical' in one sense of the word because they are a record of a judge's stated reasoning – in research terms, a bit like the transcript of an interview for a sociologist). But everyone does this; legal realists, however, also believed in the quantitative sort of empiricism.

Realism must also be understood to be a way of *doing* legal study, rather than a single view of law. Certainly, the realists held a number of things in common, not just certain methods, but method seems to be the chief feature. Rumble, though a great admirer of Llewellyn, accused him of being not fully frank in advancing the view that realism is a method,[43] but he nonetheless had to concede that realism did not have a clear and coherent content that one could point to: 'A perennial criticism of the legal realists has been their failure to formulate a "philosophy" of law.'[44]

So, what about realism and *contract* specifically? How did realism, which, after all, was an academic theory/approach, influence the way lawyers think, the way we talk about the law, what we expect to happen in the law, and the development of the actual law itself, whether in the form of legislation or, usually much more important for contract law in the common law world, in

---

41 Twining, op. cit., p.65.
42 Karl Llewellyn in an address given apparently in 1956, quoted in Twining, op. cit., p.63f, but not referenced.
43 W.E. Rumble, *American Legal Realism* (Cornell University Press: Ithaca, NY, 1968), p.35.
44 Ibid.

judicial development? This is where we need to introduce two giants of American contract law: Arthur Corbin and Karl Llewellyn.

Corbin

> **BIO NOTE**
>
> Arthur Linton Corbin was born in Linn County, Kansas, on 17 October1874. Having graduated from the University of Kansas in 1894 he taught for a while at high schools in Augusta and Lawrence, both in Kansas. He then went up to Yale Law School, graduating (*magna cum laude*) in 1899, going on to practise law in Cripple Creek, Colorado, before returning to Yale in 1903 to serve as an instructor in contracts.
>
> He became a full professor at Yale Law School in 1909 and stayed in that post until his retirement in 1943. At Yale he managed to convince the authorities to reform the Law School along lines previously adopted by Langdell at Harvard: more full-time faculty were hired, who were not necessarily practitioners, admission became more selective and Langdell's casebook teaching method was adopted.
>
> He died in 1967.

Corbin, like so many American contract scholars, had a long and distinguished career starting in what was really quite early days for the development of contract law writing in America. The main textbook at the time was still an American edition of the English contract textbook by Sir Frederick Pollock. The first volume of Samuel Williston's treatise on contracts came out in 1920, seven years after Corbin had begun his career as an academic jurist. This work has been seen as the great American statement of 'classical' contract law (or 'the classical general theory of contracts'). Corbin wrote a review on the first volume when it came out and said in it:

> The reviewer's differences with the author are nearly always with respect to definition and legal analysis, rather than with respect to decisions on specific facts. Doubtless, this might indicate that no particular terminology or method of analysis is absolutely necessary to a just and correct decision. But clear and definite concepts, accurate analysis into simple and invariable elements, a terminology that conveys to other minds the exact idea intended, are always exceedingly desirable and are often essential.[45]

45 A.L. Corbin, 'Review of Williston on Contracts – Vol. I.' (1920) 29 *Yale LJ* 942.

What seems to be in Corbin's mind here is not that contractual liability is not distinct from tortious liability,[46] or that a number of general principles governing contracts cannot be arrived at and defined in an analytical exercise, but rather that the definitions available (i.e., the pure classical theory of Williston, Pollock and Anson) inaccurately describes what those principles are. This is amply borne out in Corbin's 1926 article on consideration,[47] which is well worth reading if you get the chance.

But Corbin subsequently came to write his own great treatise on American contract law, and in that he writes about 'the illusion of certainty ... the delusion that law is absolute and eternal, that doctrines can be used mechanically, and that there are correct and unchangeable definitions'.[48] Corbin was here arguing for 'comparative historical study of cases in great number'.[49] Corbin was a convinced collector of large amounts of authority (and the West system of reporting nearly everything, as opposed to the English system of reporting only very selectively, gave a great deal of scope for this). Williston, who was Chief Reporter for the Restatement project, by way of contrast, operated more in the English style. It is not merely the quantity (and quality) of American case law that differs from English case law, but also the way in which it is used. The English approach is to draw, so far as possible, general principles from a number of decisions on specific instances. The American approach, in contrast, is characterised by the 'all fours case'; that is to say, the American lawyer typically seeks to find, amid the mass of reports available, a case on as nearly the same facts as the instant case as possible. Corbin, who was Williston's principal assistant on the Restatement, preferred the less selective approach. In the circumstances, some conflict between their conclusions was inevitable. Moreover, conclusions which Corbin might draw from a large number of cases, all accepted as correctly decided, would naturally tend toward much wider, looser statements of principle than could be achieved using Williston's technique. However, this does not necessarily mean that they would produce rules that could not live with one another. An example of this can be found in sections 75 and 90 of the Restatement, which run as follows:

Section 75 –
(1) Consideration for a promise is
    (a) an act other than a promise, or
    (b) a forbearance, or

---

46 Which, we venture to suggest, would involve a reworking of the now traditional definition of torts in terms of claims for unliquidated damages. See, generally, R.F.V. Heuston and R.A. Buckley, *Salmond & Heuston on the Law of Torts*, 21st edn (Sweet & Maxwell: London, 1996), ch.1.

47 A.L. Corbin, 'Non-Binding Promises as Consideration' (1926) 26 *Colum LR* 550.

48 A.L. Corbin, Contracts, para.109 (1963).

49 Loc. cit.

    (c) the creation, modification or destruction of a legal relation, or
    (d) a return promise, bargained for and given in exchange for the
        promise.
(2) Consideration may be given to the promisor or to some other person.
    It may be given by the promisee or by some other person.

Section 90 –

A promise which the promisor should reasonably expect to induce action
or forbearance of a definite and substantial character on the part of the
promisee and which does induce such action or forbearance is binding if
injustice can be avoided only by enforcement of the promise.

Gilmore argues[50] that these are two conflicting versions of the doctrine of
consideration: section 75 being Williston's and section 90 being Corbin's,
which was inserted after Corbin protested to the Restatement group that he
could cite hundreds, perhaps thousands, of cases in which the courts had
imposed contractual liability where they would not have done so had they been
working on the basis of the section 75 definition.

The section 90 statement, however, would look familiar to any English
lawyer today as a reasonable working definition of promissory estoppel, except
that it goes further and acts as a 'sword' and not merely as a 'shield'.[51] So it
goes rather further than the English doctrine does at present – although this
saying that promissory estoppel is a 'shield not a sword' – i.e., it can be used
to set up a promise as a defence in a case, but cannot be used as the basis for
suing someone for breach of contract – was described as a 'misleading
aphorism' by the English Court of Appeal in *Baird Textile Holdings Ltd v Marks
& Spencer plc*,[52] and as 'largely inaccurate' in *Azov Shipping Co. v Baltic Shipping
Co.*,[53] but similar ideas are at work).

It might certainly be argued that section 90 is really a US version of
promissory estoppel, going further than the English version, but the English
version itself is an attempt to get around possible injustices created by strict
application of traditional definitions of consideration (the 'practical benefit' rule
introduced by the English Court of Appeal in *Williams v Roffey Brothers & Nicholls
(Contractors) Ltd*[54] is a separate approach to other problems created by the
doctrine of consideration). In other words, the promissory estoppel doctrine
in England could really be the early stages of development of a new, wider
definition of consideration in English law that would gradually emerge over
the next few decades or centuries).

Because of Restatement section 90 and because of Cardozo's efforts in the
New York Court of Appeals, Gilmore claims Corbin and Cardozo can be

50 Gilmore, op. cit., pp.65–68.
51 See *Combe v Combe* [1951] 2 KB 215.
52 [2001] EWCA Civ 274; [2001] 1 All ER (Comm) 737 at [52].
53 [1999] 2 Lloyd's Rep 159 at 175.
54 [1991] 1 QB 1 (CA).

characterised as 'the engineers of [the general theory's] destruction'. He picks out Cardozo's judgments in *De Cicco v Schweizer*[55] and *Allegheny College v National Chautauqua Bank*[56] as examples of Cardozo finding consideration in just about any circumstance. The *Allegheny College* case is indeed difficult (although by no means impossible) to explain on traditional consideration doctrine lines, but *De Cicco* was a marriage settlement case, and there is nothing radical in finding marriage as a good consideration. To speak of Corbin and Cardozo as demolition men is a bit extreme. Gilmore was trying to justify the position that there was no separate entity as 'the law of contract', just a tort of breach of contract and lots of specialised rules for different sorts of contract. What Corbin and Cardozo appear to have been trying to do was to change some of the definitions (in Corbin's case) and the application of the rules (in Cardozo's case) to make the law in the books more accurately reflect the law in the courts and to make the law in the courts more reflective of what parties really thought they were doing and what people generally would see as 'just'.

Corbin's scepticism toward doctrine, and his preference for the facts of cases and their raw results over the opinions of judges is quite characteristic of legal realism and he surely played an important rôle in ameliorating the strictness of Ansonian and Willistonian 'classicalism', leading to what some theorists call 'neo-classical contract'. That said, the move towards the broader definitions and 'fuzzier' application of this 'neo-classical contract' (or just 'contemporary' contract) might have been inevitable: Anson and Williston belonged to an era of unquestioning belief in *laissez faire*, extreme views about the extent of free will, and an utter faith in the free market, while Corbin's career spanned the loss of confidence in the market, America's New Deal and Keynesian economics – the *political* centre of gravity changed, in other words, and led to expectations of a different approach to deciding contract disputes.

Llewellyn

The Uniform Commercial Code began with a more limited project on sales, although the people involved in the sales project mostly envisaged that it would form the core of a wider Code. This was a cooperative venture between the National Conference of Commissioners on Uniform State Laws ('NCC') and the American Law Institute ('ALI'), which began in 1942, with Llewellyn being nominated by the ALI as Chief Reporter. (They adapted their procedures from those used in producing the Restatements.) Upwards of 1,000 lawyers were ultimately involved in producing the Code, but the vital importance of the Chief Reporter and, more importantly, his opportunity to put his own theories into practice are made evident by the terms of the agreement between the

---

55   221 N.Y. 341 (1917); 117 N.E. 807.
56   246 N.Y. 369 (1927); 159 N.E. 173.

BIO NOTE

Karl Llewellyn was born on 22 May1893 in Seattle, Washington State. His boyhood was spent in Brooklyn, New York. After graduating from Yale he proceeded to Yale Law School and gained the distinction of being editor-in-chief of the *Yale Law Journal*.

Llewellyn was studying at the Sorbonne in Paris when WW I broke out in 1914. His part-German origins attracted him to the German cause so he promptly went to Germany and fought with the 78th Prussian Infantry Regiment with whom he served at First Ypres, where he was injured. After this he was he was promoted to the rank of sergeant and awarded the Iron Cross (2nd Class). After 10 weeks in a German hospital, he returned to the United States and resumed his studies at Yale in March 1915. Ironically, perhaps, Llewellyn subsequently attempted to join the US Army when America eventually entered the war but was turned down because he had fought for the Germans.

Llewellyn's academic career began at Columbia Law School in 1925. In 1951 he moved to University of Chicago Law School.

Llewellyn married Soia Mentschikoff who was also a law professor who had worked with him on drafting the Uniform Commercial Code.

Llewellyn died in Chicago on 13 February 1962.

NCC and the ALI, signed on 1 December 1944, which included the following provisions in relation to the Chief Reporter:

> The Chief Reporter shall have general supervision over the work of all other Reporters and their assistants.
>
> Subject to approval by the Editorial Board, he shall *give instructions to the Reporters as to the theory* on which drafts shall be prepared. [. . .]
>
> As ex officio member of the several Reportorial Groups, the Chief Reporter . . . shall have the right at [his] pleasure to attend any meeting of any . . . group and participate in its deliberations.[57]

It is obvious, then, that Llewellyn was in a position of the greatest possible influence, especially as to the theoretical underpinning of the jurisprudence of the Code. So, how did this influence make itself felt? The drafting of such a Code is clearly an exercise in rule making, and each section of each article

---

57 Agreement between NCC and ALI, 1 December 1944, reproduced from Twining, op. cit., pp.282–283 (emphasis added).

is a rule. Let us start, then by asking what Llewellyn thought of as good practice in rule making. William Twining identifies three ideas as to what Llewellyn thought of as 'good' rules:

1   the purpose of the rule is clearly stated in the rule itself.
2   the scope of the rule should be, so far as possible, coextensive with the purpose (i.e., the rule provides exactly what is needed and no more, to put into effect its purpose) and should be related to typical situations that often occur; and
3   the boundaries of the application are drawn in broad, general terms.[58]

We might also identify some other features of Llewellyn and realism:

- pragmatism, set against dogmatism (the supposed failing of formalists)
- the idea (from Justice Oliver Wendell Holmes Jr) that laws should reflect the morality of those governed by them
- rule scepticism (clearly an important issue for those who would make up rules)
- empiricism (a focus on available facts rather than just theories)
- grouping cases and legal situations into narrower categories than had been done in the past.

An example of the first of the 'good rule' points might be found in section 4-107, which reads as follows:

Section 4-107. Time of Receipt of Items

(1) *For the purpose of allowing time to process items*, prove balances and make the necessary entries on its books to determine its position for the day, a bank may fix an afternoon hour of two P.M. or later as a cut-off hour for the handling of money and items and the making of entries in its books.

(2) Any item or deposit of money received on any day after a cut-off hour so fixed or after the close of the banking day may be treated as being received at the opening of the next banking day.

Here the purpose of the rule is stated explicitly (the portion in italics) although, as Twining notes, 'only sparing use was made of the device of incorporating specific statements in the rules themselves'.[59] The scope of the rule is coextensive with its purpose. Finally, although it cannot really be said to be drawn in particularly 'broad, general terms', it is not overly prescriptive and allows bankers a fair amount of discretion in setting their own rules in reliance on it.

---

58 Twining, op. cit., p.326, derived from Llewellyn's *The Common Law Tradition*.
59 Twining, op. cit., p.323.

As far as pragmatism goes, we might fairly look at the form of the Code as a whole. 'Commercial law' is a slightly vague concept to begin with: what might be considered to be 'commercial law' is always arguable. For instance, is carriage of goods by sea part of 'commercial law' or part of 'maritime law'? The Code was to be functionally literate (by which we mean that, as far as what was to be included is concerned, all parts need to be shown fairly clearly to be logically connected to one another), yet broad enough in scope so that the aims of a uniform set of state laws on commercial transactions is not frustrated by differences in state laws on connected matters (securities, for example). In his memorandum concerning a '[p]ossible Uniform Commercial Code', Llewellyn described its scope as 'the *movement of goods, the payment therefor, and the financing thereof*'. The Code would also need to be reasonably digestible to businesspeople, who would need to be able to apply it without constant recourse to expert legal advice, and to identify when legal advice was really needed:

> Harmonious arrangement, simplification of language, and thorough re-thinking to eliminate all fine distinctions *which prove to have no adequate basis in policy and practice*, can tremendously ease access to commercial law, for lawyer and for layman.
>
> I do not suggest any chasing of that will o'the wisp, 'business law made plain to every layman'. I do suggest that, for instance, the very layman who is today unable to find, anywhere, an exposition intelligible to him of what a 'C.I.F.' quotation will mean to him, can make reasonable sense out of . . . the new Sales draft. He will still need a lawyer, to tell him what the effect will be, of a provision shifting the risk of an advance in freight rates to the buyer; but he will stand a much greater chance of seeing that he needs a lawyer for that purpose and also of understanding what his lawyer tells him.[60]

As Twining observes:

> [T]he Sales Article was treated as the central pillar of the Code. Secured transactions, commercial paper, bank deposits and collections and letters of credit are all functionally important for paying for and financing the flow of goods. . . . Insurance was not included . . . because some of it was politically controversial . . . [agency is left to the general law because] agency is not limited to commercial situations and the civilians have had many difficulties in fitting commercial law into the framework of the general law.[61]

---

60 Loc. cit. Italics and idiosyncratic punctuation are Llewellyn's.
61 Twining, op. cit., pp.330–331.

However, some matters that might be considered a bit tangential or marginal were included in the Code because they had been included in earlier uniform Acts that were being repealed. As Twining observed, 'the coverage of the prior uniform acts and political expediency played an important part in the determination of the scope of the Code, which can accordingly be said to have been governed by pragmatic rather than by dogmatic functionalism.'[62]

Both the value of 'empirical' research and of reflecting the morality (or at least the expectations and practices) of those governed, are reflected in the informal 'if I were a cheque' conversations Llewellyn had with NCC members, which were aimed at finding out what normal practice was. (And this is a form of empirical research – finding out what is actually done in the real world.) The evident policy of reflecting actual business practice (or at least best practice), for instance in the requirement for 'good faith', which the Code imported into ordinary commercial contract law of a major common law jurisdiction for the first time, demonstrates the Code's respect for the 'morality' of those governed by it.

Rule scepticism is harder to find, for the obvious reason that someone drafting a large number of rules might have difficulty in displaying such a quality. Nonetheless, the provisions for interpretation of the Code do suggest a view that dogmatic and formalistically applied rules are not the way in which the law is (or ought) to be administered. For instance, section 1-102(1) reads as follows: 'This Act shall be liberally construed and applied to promote its underlying purposes and policies.' Whether this really is a reflection of rule scepticism must, however, remain in doubt: the comment on section 1-102 makes clear that the purpose of providing for a liberal interpretation is to build in flexibility 'since it is intended to be a semi-permanent piece of legislation, it will provide its own machinery for . . . the law . . . to be developed by the courts in the light of unforeseen and new circumstances and practices'.[63] In other words, the 'liberal interpretation' clause is really intended to allow the development of a case law tradition on the interpretation of the Code.

This leaves the issue of grouping cases and legal situations into narrower categories than had been done in the past. Here, frankly, the whole tone of the UCC is out of keeping with this particular tenet of Llewellian realism. The sections on personal property as security, for example,[64] tend to paint the area with a *broader* brush than had previously been the case and it can be argued that one of the purposes of the Code, i.e., 'to simplify and modernise' the law would run against atomisation into many narrower categories: the tendency from the late nineteenth century onwards, mainly carried out by academic jurists has been to develop theories of law that tend to cover ever more situations under fewer, bigger umbrellas. Before this lawyers tended to think about contracts in a very atomised fashion: carriers' contracts, innkeepers'

---

62 Twining, op. cit., p.331.
63 UCC, s.1-102, comment.
64 See, generally, UCC, article 7.

contracts and so on. The unifying aspects being the *procedure* used for bringing an action for a breach of contract, as we saw in Chapter 2 when we looked at the rise of the action of *assumpsit* to provide a remedy. Lawyers knew about a single procedure and key words used in pleadings, but it was late nineteenth-century jurists such as Anson, Pollock and Langdell who insisted that contracts themselves were characterised and governed by a limited set of doctrines.

The UCC was a compromise document, however, produced in committees and requiring the assent of a variety of constituencies. It is not to be expected, therefore, that it should consistently reflect the theoretical standpoint of one man in unadulterated glory. This brief glance at its jurisprudence still indicates, however, a powerful realist current. The UCC is a fact; it *is* law. Llewellyn's influence on both academic theory and the actual substantive law, governing millions of contracts and thousands of lawsuits every year, is quite plain.

On balance, however, perhaps the most convenient summary of both Corbin's and Llewellyn's contributions is that of Ian Macneil (see Chapter 5) in his article 'Contracts: Adjustment of Long-Term Economic Relations Under Classical, Neoclassical, and Relational Contract Law', in which he writes:

> Classical contract law refers (in American terms) to that developed in the 19th century and brought to its pinnacle by Samuel Williston in *The Law of Contracts* (1920) and in the Restatement of Contracts (1932). Neoclassical contract law refers to a body of contract law founded on that system in overall structure but considerably modified in some, although by no means all, of its detail. The latter is epitomized by the U.C.C. Art. 2, and Restatement (Second) of Contracts.[65]

Fuller

Fuller is best known for the article he wrote with his student, William R. Perdue Jr for the *Yale Law Journal* in 1933,[66] which argued the reliance basis for contract enforcement as against what Fried has called 'contract as promise'. This was described by Atiyah as 'probably . . . the most influential single article in the entire history of modern contract scholarship'.[67] Its novelty might best be judged in the light of Williston's comment 12 years earlier that:

> [T]he fundamental idea on which the action of assumpsit and the development of simple contracts rested, was that reliance on a promise – the reliance being induced by the promisor's request of an act or counter-promise of the other party – caused an obligation to arise.[68]

---

65 (1978) 72 *Northwestern L.R.* 854 at 855, n.2.
66 L. Fuller and W.R. Perdue Jr, 'The Reliance Interest in Contract Damages' (1933) 46 *Yale L.J.* 52, and 373.
67 Sir P.S. Atiyah, *Essays on Contract* (Clarendon Press: Oxford, 1988), p.73.
68 In S. Williston, 'Freedom of Contract' (1921) 6 Cornell LQ 365, reproduced in AALS, *Selected Readings on the Law of Contracts* (Macmillan: New York, 1931), p.103 at pp.103–104.

Another great US contracts scholar, Ames, also noted the importance of reliance, or 'detriment' (and the fact that Langdell took the same view):

> Consideration, according to the traditional definition is either a detriment incurred by the promisee or a benefit received by the promisor in exchange for the promise. Professor Langdell has pointed out the irrelevancy of the notion of benefit to the promisor, and makes detriment to the promisee the universal test of consideration. The simplified definition has met with much favor . . . In one respect only does the definition leave anything to desire. What is to be understood by detriment?[69]

We have already seen in Chapter 2 that the modern law of contract grew from the medieval actions of debt and *assumpsit*. Therefore, since the rôle of reliance in *assumpsit* was already recognised by those arch-classicalists Langdell, Williston and Ames, we need probably say little more about it. Perhaps its significance is really that it brought a particular view of the basis of contract to far greater prominence than an essentially historical note in a four-volume treatise or a paragraph or two in a paper on freedom of contract, by bringing out the issue, alone, on the accessible stage of a law review article. If reliance is the basis, then one might, in a sense, commit a contract much as one commits a tort: having induced someone else's reliance on us, we are duty bound to ensure that they do not thereby lose because of our default, be it misfeasance or nonfeasance. Here, perhaps, are the seeds of the 'death of contract' movement, which denied the accuracy and utility of classical contract theory, asserted that contract can be treated as an obligation akin to any tort (indeed, in the sixteenth century many actions in *assumpsit* were only brought on the *assumpsit* because that would allow the recovery of sums paid in advance for services negligently rendered, where most of the damage was such as could be recovered in an action on the case for negligence), and thought there were better things to do with one's time and one's students' time than study the general theory of contracts – such as studying sociology.[70]

It might be that Fuller's 1941 article, 'Consideration as Form'[71] is more important from the standpoint of tracing the development of contract theory in the twentieth century. The idea that consideration (the requirement for a *quid pro quo* to make a promise enforceable) is only the same sort of thing as formality (e.g., a deed, a written contract, a signature, or some sort of ceremonial) goes against traditional understandings of consideration as the very basis of enforcement of promises not under seal. To quote from Williston again:

69 J.B. Ames, 'Two Theories of Consideration', (1899) 12 *Harvard LR* 515.
70 Gilmore, op. cit., p 3.
71 (1941) 41 *Colum LR* 799.

There was but little discussion or theorizing about mutual assent in the cases on assumpsit until nearly the end of the eighteenth century; and the basis of the action was conceived to be consideration rather than the mutual will of the parties.[72]

Also, when what we are really looking for is the *outward appearance* of agreement, as in the objective test of agreement for which the classic cases are *Smith v Hughes*[73] in England and *Bohn Manufacturing Co. v Sawyer*[74] in America (approved by no less a figure than Holmes CJ in *Spencer v Spencer*[75]) rather than on *actual* agreement of inward intentions, we return, as Williston said,[76] to an older theory, where assent is simply not the point. What matters is the proof of consideration as a sort of test of whether the plaintiff was entitled to rely on the defendant's promise.

The 'death of contract'

This final section of this chapter is really a sort of footnote to the preceding story. In 1957 a symposium was held at the University of Wisconsin. The general theme and upshot of this was the view that 'contract' meaning the classical or neo-classical system of the law of contract, not the phenomenon of contracting as such or of adjudication by the courts on breaches of contract, was dead. It was said that really breaching a contract was simply a wrong like other wrongs – a tort, in fact. Like other torts, it had its special requirements and incidents, but the idea that contracts existed as a special entity and were constituted and governed by fixed principles applying to all contracts, such as the requirements for agreement, for there to be consideration or form, intention to create legal relations, and so on – all the things we think of when we think of 'the law of contract' – was false. The whole structure was an academic construct.

Of course, there was some truth in this. There was nothing absolutely new in what the English and American contracts scholars had identified – the courts had been talking about consideration for centuries, about agreement for more than half a century, for example, but the elegant interconnected structure was an academic 'discovery'. Quite how that makes it illegitimate is not clear – lots of areas of human knowledge have only been made sense of by academic organisation. Be that as it may, the post-Wisconsin 'death of contract' school believed that we could not legitimately study contract as legal doctrine, but only engage in sociological study of contracting as a form of human behaviour.

72 Loc. cit., *supra*, n.48.
73 (1871) L.R. 6 Q.B. 597.
74 169 Mass. 477.
75 181 Mass. 471.
76 Williston, *supra*, n.48.

The term 'death of contract' has come to be specially associated with the name of Grant Gilmore, because he published a book of that title, containing the text of a series of public lectures he gave at Ohio State University in 1973. Gilmore actually repudiated the idea of sociological study, but it is far from clear on reading this book (by all means try this) what he *would* study. The book itself seems on the face of it to be a rather snide and spiteful attack on successive leading figures at Harvard Law School. The book's account of the history of the classical general theory of contracts has been very influential over the succeeding four decades, but it is a highly misleading account, as we have seen earlier.

The fuss surrounding this book and the reputation that Gilmore already had, rather overshadowed the birth of relational contract theory (the subject of Chapter 5 of this book), which may have been its greatest real effect, and perhaps quite a damaging one – but you can judge for yourself on that one.

Suggested further reading

C. Fried, *Contract as Promise* (Harvard University Press: Cambridge, MA, 1981).

L. Fuller and W.R. Perdue Jr, 'The Reliance Interest in Contract Damages' (1933) 46 *Yale LJ* 52, 373.

G. Gilmore, *The Death of Contract* (Ohio State University Press: Columbus, OH, 1974).

W.E. Rumble, *American Legal Realism* (Cornell University Press: Ithaca, NY, 1968).

R.E. Speidel, 'An Essay on the Reported Death and Continued Vitality of Contract' (1975) *Stanford LR* 1161.

W. Twining, *Karl Llewellyn and the Realist Movement* (Weidenfeld & Nicholson: London, 1973).

4 The ideological context of contract

- Introduction
- Formalism
- Realism
- Market-individualism
- Consumer-welfarism

Introduction

In this chapter, when we speak of ideology we are not referring to, say, capitalism as opposed to socialism. Rather, we mean two particular pairs of competing ideologies. One pair identifies two contrasting approaches to adjudication in any kind of legal dispute. We call these 'formalism' and 'realism' and you have already come across these ideas in Chapter 3. The other pair identifies two ideologies relating specifically to contract, not to the law in general. We call these 'market-individualism' and 'consumer-welfarism'. This short chapter aims to explain the basic features of each of these four ideologies and to show how the two pairs intersect with and affect each other. In doing this, the authors of this book rest very heavily on another book that has long been put into the hands of law students in England: *Understanding Contract Law* by Professor Roger Brownsword and the late Professor John Adams.[1]

A good starting point would be to stress that the adjudication ideologies (formalism and realism) can each intersect (that is be combined with) either of the contract ideologies. But the two adjudication ideologies cannot combine with one another, and the two contract ideologies likewise cannot combine with each other (see Table 4.1).

---

1 J.N. Adams and R. Brownsword, *Understanding Contract Law*, 5th edn (Sweet & Maxwell: London, 2007).

Table 4.1 Intersections and non-intersections of ideologies.

Contract/adjudication ideologies	Formalism	Realism
Market-individualism	Formalism/market-individualism	Realism/market-individualism
Consumer-welfarism	Formalism/consumer-welfarism	Realism/consumer-welfarism

Now some explanation of what we mean by these terms and examples of how they might be seen to operate in practice. We shall begin with formalism and realism, the general ideologies of adjudication (which are also approaches to studying and writing about law), before moving on to consider the contract-specific ideologies of market-individualism and consumer-welfarism. In this chapter (note – not necessarily elsewhere in the book), we will use the terms as Adams and Brownsword use them in *Understanding Contract Law.*

Formalism

Formalism is, in essence, what is called 'the rulebook' approach. The idea is that any problem presenting itself to the common law judge can be resolved by the accurate identification and proper application of known and established rules, whether statutory or judicially discovered ones.

The rulebook, certainly in relation to contract law, is a complete, standalone, logical system. Select the right rule and apply it correctly and the outcome *must* be right. Sometimes the result may seem harsh (or frankly idiotic) but that does not matter: it is still right. If the rule is considered too harsh or perverse, then it is for the legislature to intervene through legislative change. One is reminded a little of Sherlock Holmes explaining to Dr Watson that once one has eliminated the impossible, whatever remains, however improbable, must be the right answer. Formalism is an approach applicable to all areas of law, but few are so perfectly systematised as contracts. The selection of actions that we group together and call torts, for instance, has no real underlying plan, although one could hang them together by saying that they are non-contractual civil wrongs that carry a remedy at common law of unliquidated (i.e., plucked out of the air by the judge or jury rather than arithmetically calculated) damages. Nevertheless, each individual tort has its own system, its own relentless logic. It is probably fair to say that most first-year law students are realists trapped inside formalists: they like the notions of 'justice' and 'fairness', but they are even more convinced that there simply must be one correct legal rule to apply to any given situation that will infallibly produce a legally 'correct' result. This often results in disappointment and some confusion when a tutor refuses to specify a 'right answer' to a hypothetical case in a 'problem question'.

This approach also gives rise to the maxim that 'hard cases make bad law'. What this means is that if you get a case where the rule appears to point to a solution that might appear unjust on the merits of the case – evil corporation gets to oppress hapless poor person, say – one should accept this 'hard' outcome. To try to do justice in the individual case by making some exception to the rule, thereby changing the rulebook, is likely to result in either future cases being decided in accordance with the exception even though the merits would suggest another outcome – so the modified rule produces negative effects in other cases – or else the rulebook becomes loaded with a plague of *ad hoc* exceptions which stand outside any logical scheme. There is some merit in this argument, whatever the deficiencies of formalism in general might be.

Adams and Brownsword give the example of Lawton LJ's remarks in the famous English 'battle of the forms' case, *Butler Machine Tool Co Ltd v Ex-Cell-O Corporation (England) Ltd*:

> The problem is how should that battle be conducted? The view taken by the [trial] judge was that the battle should extend over a wide area and the court should do its best to look into the minds of the parties and make certain assumptions. In my judgment, the battle has to be conducted in accordance with set rules . . . The rules relating to a battle of this kind have been known for the past 130-odd years.[2]

Actually the problem was a relatively new one – of companies trying to deal with each other, each using its own printed forms with its own standard terms on the back: company A asks company B for a quotation for a product or service, company B replies using a printed 'Quotation' form with its 'Terms & Conditions' printed on the back. Company A then responds with an order on its printed 'Purchase Requisition' form with its own, different, 'Terms & Conditions' on the back. Company B then responds with its 'Sales Confirmation' form with its original terms on the back and so on. What Lawton LJ meant was that the rules for working out when offer and acceptance had occurred and therefore on what terms the contract was made were well-established ones. A 'battle of the forms' was nothing special – the ordinary rules could be applied to settle this kind of case as well.

It is also important in formalism that what Adams and Brownsword describe as 'conceptual purity' of the rulebook be maintained. The doctrines should all fit together with one another and 'deviant' doctrines should be kept out. An example of where our rulebook is not internally consistent is that of the rule against penalties, where a court refuses to enforce a clause in a contract stipulating the damages payable in the event of breach. This goes against the doctrine of 'freedom of contract' (that parties are free to enter into a contract with each other on whatever terms they like – the business of the court is to

---

2 [1979] 1 All ER 965 (CA) at 969.

enforce the contract the parties have made, not act as a sort of nanny, demanding that they play nicely). This rule has caused much pain to contract law professors around the whole common law world.

Formalists tend to be doctrinal conservatives – they do not like new ideas creeping into the law and if one does slip in they try to narrow the scope of its operation as far as possible, hoping one day to get rid of it altogether. A good example of this, we think, is the effective abolition of the doctrine of equitable mistake by the English Court of Appeal in *The Great Peace*.[3] Formalists are suspicious of 'policy' considerations affecting a court's judgment, which links to the sanctity and infallibility of the rulebook in the same way as the problem of 'hard cases'. Formalists prefer clear general rules and prefer to minimise or eliminate judicial discretion (which is not the same thing as the exercise of judgment and decision).

Realism

We have already defined realism in Chapter 3, but we are going to define it again because: (a) you might be dipping into this book and not have read Chapter 3 yet; (b) you might have read Chapter 3 but forgotten what we said about realism; and (c) we are being specific in this chapter about using 'realism' in the way Adams and Brownsword use the term in their book, which is more about a judicial approach to deciding cases rather than about an academic approach to studying law (with or without legislative consequences), as with the description of legal realism given in Chapter 3.

Adams and Brownsword characterise realism in adjudication as follows. First, the rulebook is not decisive. Adjudications are (or should be) driven by the facts (merits) of the case and where formalism is driven by rules, realism is 'result oriented'. As an example of this approach, they cite Lord Devlin's observation in *Ingram v Little* that: 'The true spirit of the common law is to override theoretical distinctions when they stand in the way of doing practical justice.'[4] *Ingram v Little* was a case in which two dear old ladies were diddled out of their car by a rogue in circumstances frankly indistinguishable from those in which a jeweller was parted from his wares by a fraudster in *Phillips v Brooks*,[5] which ended badly for the jeweller, whereas in *Ingram v Little*, the old ladies succeeded against the apparent authority of the earlier case (which was, however, in a lower court). It certainly looks like a case in which judicial sympathy for one party overrode the value of predictability in the law. (It should be stressed, by the way, that the old ladies were not suing the rogue, but rather the entirely innocent used car dealer who bought the car from the rogue.)

3 [2002] EWCA Civ 1407; [2003] QB 679.
4 [1961] 1 QB 31 (CA) at 66.
5 [1919] 2 KB 243 (KBD).

A realist judge, they say, will sometimes disregard the logic of the rulebook conceptualisation of contract as with Lord Denning in *Gibson v Manchester City Council*,[6] or at least to circumvent it by cunning means, as the House of Lords did in *Beswick v Beswick*.[7] It follows also that the realist does not really mind messing up the rulebook with *ad hoc* exceptions and conceptual fudging.

Realism 'tends towards doctrinal and conceptual innovation', say Adams and Brownsword,[8] giving as examples the doctrines of promissory estoppel, unconscionability, economic duress and innominate terms. Moreover, they suggest that the realist judge will be happy to put forward a new or recently stated theory or doctrine to support a particular decision rather than seeking a traditional basis for making a decision. You might like to look at the case of *Williams v Roffey Brothers & Nicholls (Contractors) Ltd*,[9] to see judges using an idea they have just made up to decide a case and think about whether you could have reached the same result by cunning use of more traditional reasoning. Contrariwise, while Adams and Brownsword cite a number of examples of Lord Denning adopting a realist approach, there are plenty of examples of his digging up old and sometimes obscure cases to show that he was not innovating at all (even if, actually, he was): consider the then Denning J's use of *Hughes v Metropolitan Railway Co.*[10] in his judgment in *Central London Property Trust Ltd v High Trees House Ltd*.[11] For the realist judge, also, sympathy for a party and policy considerations both matter and should affect the outcome of the case. They are less affected by the consideration that 'hard cases make bad law' and are more heavily influenced by the merits of the case in hand.

The 'mechanical and uncritical adoption and application of the rule-book'[12] is rejected by realist judges. Rules are examined to determine their original purpose. If a particular rule no longer serves, perhaps even frustrates that original purpose, then it is time for a change. Moreover, changing social attitudes and common values may require new purposes to be pursued by the courts and new doctrines to achieve them. Judicial discretion is not necessarily considered to be problematic. Discretion gives a judge the opportunity to take into account factors leading to conclusions supporting the decision they want to reach.

Finally, realist appellate judges see the rôle of an appellate court more widely than formalists would tend to. A formalist looks to an appellate tribunal to consider whether there was any fault in the way in which a lower court reached the decision it did. If fault cannot be found, then the appeal is refused, even

---

6 [1978] 2 All ER 583 (CA).
7 [1968] AC 58.
8 Op. cit., p.191.
9 [1991] 1 QB 1 (CA).
10 (1876–77) LR 2 App. Cas. 439 (HL).
11 [1947] KB 130 (KBD).
12 Adams and Brownsword, op. cit., p.191.

if the appellate court might have reached a different conclusion by other processes of reasoning than those adopted below. The realist sees in an appeal the opportunity to assess the overall effect of the decision below and whether that seems to that court to be satisfactory. Whether this is a good thing or not depends, of course, on your point of view. A powerful argument against this approach can be found in the fact that the trial judge, at any rate, has the opportunity of hearing all the evidence, observing witnesses and so on. An even more powerful argument, perhaps, is that in a system in which appellate courts took this wider, 'realist', view, whoever has deeper pockets will be tempted to keep appealing until they get the result they want. Adams and Brownsword comment that 'not only do realist judges put results before rules, they put pragmatism ahead of conceptual purity',[13] which sounds great, but you should not forget that there are strong counter-arguments to this sort of approach to adjudication. Legal realism as an academic tool of analysis is immensely powerful and has little potential to do harm – that is not necessarily also true of realism as a judicial decision-making method.

Table 4.2 summarises the difference between the two ideologies of adjudication, as defined by Adams and Brownsword.

Table 4.2 Difference between the two ideologies of adjudication, as defined by Adams and Brownsword

Formalism	*Realism*
Rulebook governs	Rulebook not decisive
Rule-oriented decision making	Result-oriented decision making
Rulebook is a closed logical system and the judge's job is an exercise in inexorable logic	Rulebook logic not 'be all and end all'
Rulebook's conceptual purity and integrity must be maintained	Pragmatic approach – conceptual purity less important than whether a 'rule' works
Tendency to doctrinal conservatism	Tendency to doctrinal innovation.
Sympathy for parties and policy considerations are not material	Sympathy and policy are material considerations
Rulebook uncritically accepted and mechanically applied	Purposive and critical approach to rules
Clear rules with minimal/no scope for judicial discretion or fudging	Discretion – yes please!
Not for judges to reform the law in any major way	Activist approach to law reform
Narrow view of job of appellate tribunals	Wide view of job of appellate tribunals

13 Ibid, p.192.

So much for the general – not contract law-specific – ideologies of adjudication. Now we must turn to the intersecting ideologies from Figure 4.1. Remember, these *are* specific to contract law analysis.

Market-individualism

Adams and Brownsword explain that market-individualism has two distinguishable strands to it: 'the market ideology' and the 'individualistic ideology'.[14] The market ideology does not require a belief in unfettered free markets where anything goes. Markets require rules of the game in order to function effectively and efficiently for participants. For instance, if a consumer cannot rely on some basic rights, then he may be much less willing to make purchases of non-necessities and may also engage in expensive and time-consuming investigations, which are likely also to affect the seller. If a trader cannot rely on certain assumptions as to the performance to be expected of a fellow trader, then similar costs will arise as between them. If trade customs are not respected and enforced, then contracting would need to be done in more elaborate detail, with consequential cost. A regulated market is necessary. The debate among 'free marketeers' is not whether there should be regulation but rather what is the optimal type and amount of regulation.

In the context of analysing contract law, and of adjudicating contract disputes, the market ideology claims contract law's 'function is to establish a regulated marketplace in which contractors are able to deal with security and confidence'.[15] Indeed, what distinguishes those who tend to favour freer markets is that they tend to see contract law (along with properly perceived self-interest) as the best way to regulate the market, rather than setting up elaborate regulatory regimes policed by governmental bodies.

The market ideology tends towards keeping quite a high level of freedom to bargain competitively and to take advantage of, say, differences in knowledge (often called 'informational asymmetry'), where one party knows more about the background facts and the product and so on than the other and can use that knowledge gap to his advantage in striking a deal. Hence, in most common law countries there is not a duty on one party to 'show his cards' to the other. For example, to have an action for misrepresentation, a party must show that the other party made a false statement, whether in words or by conduct (see *Spice Girls Ltd v Aprilia World Service BV*);[16] mere silence as to something the other party is likely to find relevant is not actionable.

The individualistic ideology favours self-reliance over inter-reliance. In other words, contracting parties look out for their own interests and are under no special duties to worry about what is good for the other party. This does

14   Op. cit., pp. 92 and 194, respectively.
15   Ibid., p.192.
16   [2002] EWCA Civ 15; [2002] EMLR 27 (CA).

not give them a licence to cheat and steal – rules against that (like the rules on misrepresentation) are in no way contrary to the individualistic ideology – but they are not obliged to ensure that the contract is fair or mutually advantageous. If each party looks out for its own interests effectively, then the result should be, on balance, acceptable, but woe betide the careless or ignorant party, who faces coming into the market like a lamb coming to the slaughter.

This does not mean that contracting parties do not quite often look to ensure that the other party has a satisfactory relationship – if they do, then they are less motivated to breach or otherwise seek to exit the contract and they are more likely to want to do business again in the future. This is all commercial commonsense and we shall see in Chapter 5 how these things play their part in the understandings of relational contract theory. But these factors provide relational glue holding the contractual relationship together. It is not the business – from the point of view of the individualist ideology – of contract law to provide this glue where it is otherwise lacking. (Neither does relational theory require that the law should do so: misunderstanding this point is what has led a number of contract scholars to see the decision in *Baird Textile Holdings Ltd v Marks & Spencer plc*[17] as being in conflict with the relationalist view of contract.)

In the individualistic view, the parties should be free to make what deals they wish. It is then the job of the court to enforce (by way, usually, of compensatory awards) whatever deal they did in fact make. Individualism gives us the twin ideas of 'freedom of contract' (parties are free to enter into contracts with whom they will and on what terms they happen to agree) and 'sanctity of contract' (the court will uphold the contracts the parties make and will not interfere with their terms). It will be obvious to you that individualism is only relative in practice, since in every jurisdiction there is some interference in both of these concepts. For example, the legislature might intervene making certain types of term unenforceable or of limited or contingent enforceability, as in the case of exclusion and limitation clauses in England and Wales under the Unfair Contract Terms Act 1977. Or the legislature might impose terms into contracts, as with the implied terms in various sale of goods legislation, beginning with the English Sale of Goods Act 1893 (now 1979). Similarly, the common law may interfere, but this always seems to be in ways that get around the objections of individualism. So, a court may imply terms into a contract, but these are ousted by contrary express terms in the contract and are said to express the unstated real intentions of the parties (which is likely to be true in some cases but not really true in others). Where the common law declines to enforce contracts at all – as with, for example, those connected with prostitution – it does so on the theory that they are void for reasons of morality or public

17   [2001] EWCA Civ 274; [2002] 1 All ER (Comm) 737 (CA).

policy. This does not, supposedly, offend against the doctrine of sanctity of contract because the court has characterised the arrangement as not a valid contract at all!

Consumer-welfarism

'Be nice to the little guy' sums up the underlying idea of consumer-welfarism rather well. It is too simplistic, of course, but like most generalisations it has an element of truth and an element of usefulness. The idea can be said to reflect trends towards more regulated markets that have been developing over a long period. A good example is that of the terms that the courts have implied into the employment contract. Austen-Baker in his *Implied Terms in English Contract Law*[18] cites extensive examples of terms in employment contracts in his chapter on specific instances of terms implied at common law. It is instructive to note that terms laying duties on employees, or absolving employers of duties, long predate any finding of implied terms in favour of the employee. Instances cited include one in 1858 that an employee impliedly warrants to his employer that he is reasonably skilled (*Harmer v Cornelius*)[19] and in 1893 that the employee has a duty of fidelity to his employer (*Lamb v Evans*)[20] but it is 1951 by the time a term is implied that the employer will not require an employee to commit unlawful acts (*Gregory v Ford*),[21] 1994 before the duty to take care in giving references was recognised by the English courts in *Spring v Guardian Assurance plc*,[22] and 1997 before the employer is held to owe a duty of trust and confidence to an employee (*Malik v Bank of Credit and Commerce International SA (in Liquidation)*).[23] A notable comment is that of Lord Hoffmann in *Johnson v Unisys Ltd*:

> [O]ver the last 30 years or so, the nature of the contract of employment has been transformed. It has been recognised that a person's employment is usually one of the most important things in his or her life. It gives not only a livelihood but an occupation, an identity and a sense of self-esteem. The law has changed to recognise this social reality.[24]

This more protective attitude to employees, and similarly to consumers, is characteristic of the consumer-welfarist position. But consumer-welfarism is

---

18 R. Austen-Baker, *Implied Terms in English Contract Law* (Edward Elgar: Cheltenham and Northampton, MA, 2011).
19 [1843] All ER Rep 624; (1858) 5 CBNS 236 (CP).
20 [1893] 1 Ch 218 (CA).
21 [1951] 1 All ER 121 (Assizes).
22 [1995] 2 AC 296.
23 [1998] AC 20.
24 [2001] UKHL 13; [2003] 1 AC 519 at [35].

not just about being nice. In Britain (and doubtless in some other common law jurisdictions), the state has rolled back some of its provision. Whether the provision of goods and services through nationalised industry has been dispensed with through privatisation processes or the provision of (usually) services through the welfare and other government systems has been cut back from reasons of cost, the state is a less important actor in the provision of everyday goods and services, placing more of an emphasis on the individual consumer contracting for these goods and services for him or herself. This has made it more important that consumers are protected and can secure value for money, otherwise they may lack the confidence to contract, leading to economic harms, social harms and possibly unrest or radical political shifts.

Adams and Brownsword enumerate 11 principles of consumer-welfarism,[25] although they say that even these are not exhaustive. You might want to read about these for yourself in their book, but put extremely briefly as a list, they are:

1   Reasonable reliance – a contracting party should be able to rely on the expectations generated by the other party.
2   Remedies for breach should be proportionate.
3   A principle of good faith (and remedies for bad faith).
4   No one should profit from his/her own wrong.
5   No party, even if innocent, should be unjustly enriched at another's expense.
6   Losses should usually be borne by the party better able to bear them.
7   Stronger parties should not be allowed to exploit the other party's weaker bargaining position.
8   Consumers should get a fair deal.
9   If a party making a representation has superior information then s/he should stand by their representations. But where equal information is held, there is no special case for protection.
10 Contractors at fault should be held liable – scope for exemption/limitation should be limited.
11 The law should be paternalistic, protecting the poor and ignorant (or foolish) from the negative consequences of bad bargains.

Summary

Adams and Brownsword offer a way in which to analyse and understand judgments of courts in contract cases through categorising them as falling (or tending to fall) into one of four boxes, where general ideologies of adjudication, realism and formalism, intersect with contract-specific ideologies of

25 Op. cit., pp.198–201.

Table 4.3 One way of resolving contrary tendencies between ideologies.

	Formalist	*Realist*
Market-individualist	*Philips v Brooks*	*Williams v Roffey*
Consumer-welfarist	*Thornton v Shoe Lane Parking*	*Ingram v Little*

adjudication, namely market-individualism and consumer-welfarism. One can also use this analysis to look at a particular jurisdiction compared with others, or a jurisdiction over time (as we have done really briefly in this chapter in relation to employment cases in England) or to the work of particular judges. It must come with the warning, however, that particular jurisdictions will show contrary tendencies between different cases and one judge may seem formalistic in one case but realist in another or market-individualist in one case and consumer-welfarist in another and even in the decision of one appellate court, the different judges may take different attitudes. These limitations do not make the analysis less useful or interesting, however.

We have slotted four cases each into one of the four slots available. Have a look at those cases and see if you agree with our allocation – and if not, why not? You might also like to try doing this for yourself with cases of your own choosing. Table 4.3 shows how we have resolved it.

Suggested further reading

J. Adams and R. Brownsword, *Understanding Contract Law*, 5th edn (Sweet & Maxwell: London, 2007).

[Any edition of Adams and Brownsword you can lay your hands on will do – the author of this chapter just happened to have the 5th edition to hand. See also, on legal realism, Chapter 3 of this book and the further reading list at the end of it.]

5 The relational context of contract

- Ian Macneil
- Relations v discrete transactions
- Scotch eggs and haggises – focusing on different contexts of contracts
- The norms of contract
- Practical use of relational theory

Ian Macneil

BIO NOTE

Ian R. Macneil is one of the biggest names in modern American contract theory. After a BA majoring in sociology at the University of Vermont, he went to Harvard Law School (with an interruption for WW II), and then, after some time in practice, he became an academic at the Ivy League Cornell University from 1959 to1980 (with a short interlude at the University of Virginia). In 1980 he became John Henry Wigmore Professor of Law at Northwestern University in Chicago, and remained so until his retirement in 1999. While at Harvard he was taught by the famous Lon Fuller (see Chapter 3). He was also hereditary Chief of the Clan Macneil, gifted his crofting estate on Barra to the Scottish government and granted a 1,000-year lease of his castle to Historic Scotland for a rent of one bottle of Talisker malt whisky a year. He died in February 2010.

To adopt the language of management studies, Ian Macneil was something of a 'guru'. With Stewart Macaulay, he was responsible for the development of relational contract theory, the first big thing since 'death of contract' (see Chapter 3 and below).

The two big influences on Macneil, academically speaking, were Lon Fuller and his attempt to escape from traditional contract theory, and Macneil's own participation in Rudolph Schlesinger's project on the comparative law of offer and acceptance (the results of which have long since slipped into decent obscurity). In the summer of 1964, Macneil worked on trying to find some coherent principles in contract law behind hundreds of American cases on so-called 'agreements to agree' (look up this problem in your contracts textbook). He came to the conclusion that they simply could not be made to fit what he calls 'neo-classical contract theory', in other words, the law as stated in the textbooks: it seemed to him that in many American cases the courts had in fact upheld the validity of agreements to agree, contrary to the orthodox textbook position.

All this led him to search for a new way of explaining contracts and contract law. The new way he found is what is known as 'relational contract theory'. In this chapter, we shall try to explain this theory in accessible terms, and to explore how one can use it to understand contract law better, to analyse contract rules, and to discuss proposed law reform in the field of contracts.

It should also be remembered that when he was introducing this theory, the big idea at the time was that of 'the death of contracts'. According to this theory, the whole idea of a single theory to account for contracts, such as neo-classical contract theory, was invalid: there was no such thing as a law of contract, rather there were hundreds of different, essentially unconnected, types of contract, each of which could only be explained in terms of specialised rules (e.g., for employment contracts, sales of goods contracts, charterparties, house contents insurance contracts). The leading name associated with this idea was Grant Gilmore, Sterling Professor of Law at Yale University, but he was not the inventor of the idea, although he was seen as a sort of guru for this school of thought.

KEY TERMS

Classical contract

The idea that all contracts could be explained in terms of common rules applying to them (e.g., as to offer and acceptance, intention, and consideration), and also a particular way of expressing those rules involving a strong line in favour of ideas like freedom of contract and sanctity of contracts, and defining contract rules in very narrow terms, to be applied strictly and formalistically. This characterised the approach of earlier textbook writers such as Sir William Anson and Sir Frederick Pollock in England, and Samuel Williston in America.

Neo-classical contract

Basically the same idea, but with rules drawn more broadly and fuzzily, giving greater scope to judges to rationalise the decisions they want to reach on the perceived justice of the case, and with less emphasis on freedom of contract (so as to protect the vulnerable, who might use their freedom to make undesirable contracts) and much less on sanctity of contracts. This would be a fair way to characterise most modern contract textbooks' approach.

Death of contract

The belief that classical/neo-classical contract has had its day as a way of understanding contracts and should be replaced with a nihilistic belief in contracts as hundreds of specialised entities. It may also involve a belief that a breach of contract is best regarded as another tort, like negligence or libel. This theory is now dead.

Relations v discrete transactions

When we think of contracts, we tend to think of a 'deal'. Either it is a simple exchange, like buying something in a shop, or else we think of parties negotiating over something, then agreeing terms (price, specifications, delivery time and so on), giving birth to a contract. In this case, we probably think of a contract as an entity in itself – the deal we have made, perhaps a written document detailing the terms. We might look at what the terms of the contract are, and whether each party has carried out its part of the contract. We think of the contract, then, as a *transaction*. We think of it, moreover, as a *discrete* transaction. In other words, we see it separately from anything else going on in the world at the time. It is something distinct and different and identifiable within clear parameters. When we think like this about planning a contract we are going to make, we also tend to try and think of everything important about the contract ('what happens if') and to make provision now for events that may or may not happen in the future when the contract is to be performed. Macneil calls this *'presentiation'*, meaning to make something belonging to another time present to us now. We try in the present to dictate events in the future.

Macneil encourages us to look at contracts as *relations*. That is to say, we must not see them merely as discrete events or transactions, but also in a broader context – the links between the contractual relation and society as a whole (for instance, can a contract be viable if it goes against the values of the society to which the parties belong?) and as an ongoing process with a life of its own, which grows and changes like we do in the rest of our lives.

KEY TERMS

Transaction (or 'discrete transaction')

A contract seen as a one-off event, separate from other contracts, its business, economic or social context, even from the people making the contract.

Presentiation

The attempt at providing for future contingencies by agreeing about them in the here and now (i.e., when we make a contract).

Although, in his best-known article, 'The Many Futures of Contracts',[1] he considered that there were essentially two types of contract – the contractual relation and the discrete transaction – Macneil gradually moved to the view that *all* contracts were in fact relations, and it was impossible to have such a thing as a truly discrete contract, even in theory. His famous example is of a purchase of petrol. A motorist stops at a petrol station on a road he has never been on before, and will never drive along again. He fills his car and pays for his petrol, with very little said on either side between him and an attendant he has never met before and will never meet again. Macneil says that even this is not a truly discrete transaction, because there is a whole bundle of understandings affecting the transaction that comes from the fact that they are both members of a society. The motorist is free to choose how much petrol to buy, and of what type, if there is a choice, and he also understands that he must pay for the petrol, not just drive off after filling up. The attendant also recognises that the bank notes offered in payment by the motorist are acceptable as a means of transferring value from one person to another, and also understands that if they represent more than the price of the petrol, he must give change. He also realises that he is not supposed to pull out a gun and shoot the motorist, which would also defeat the point of the transaction. Thus, both parties depend on shared assumptions, coming from the society to which they belong, in carrying through this simple transaction. Thus, it is not wholly discrete, but comes about within a wider context.

Macneil sees contracts as falling along a spectrum from the *almost* discrete to the highly relational. At the almost discrete end, we find transactions such as the petrol purchase, or, say, a commodity broker buying oil on the spot

---

1 I.R. Macneil, 'The Many Futures of Contract' (1974) 47 *Southern California L.R.* 691.

market. At the highly relational end we find, say, long-term employment contracts in highly responsible positions. The longer term the relation is, then the nearer it is likely to be to the highly relational end. The more the personality of the individual is involved, the closer it is likely to be to the highly relational end. The greater the number of people/organisations involved, the closer it is likely to be to the highly relational end. And so on.

In 'The Many Futures of Contract', Macneil expands on this idea through a discussion of a number of axes (we could call them 'spectra'), each extending from extremely transactional contracts at one end to highly relational contracts at the other, with each axis detailing features to be expected of contracts at the two poles, when viewed in different ways. Macneil proposes 12 axes in all.

MACNEIL'S AXES

1 Overall relationship type.
2 Measurability and actual measurement.
3 Basic sources of socioeconomic support.
4 Duration.
5 Commencement and termination.
6 Planning.
7 Degree of future cooperation required in post-commencement planning and performance.
8 Incidence of benefits and burdens.
9 Obligations undertaken.
10 Transferability.
11 Number of participants.
12 Participant views.

We need not examine all of these here (you can look at them for yourself in 'Many Futures'; see Figures 5.1, 5.2 and 5.3), but it would be useful to look at a few of them in order to understand better the qualities of contracts as explained by relational contract theory. As we consider these axes, *it is important to remember* that even 'highly transactional' contracts are still, in Macneil's view, relational: a 'pure' transaction is said to be impossible for the reasons discussed in the petrol purchase example just given, i.e., there are always tacit assumptions, which provide a relational backdrop to every contract.[2]

---

2 'Many Futures', p. 773, n.235

Highly transactional ⟷	Highly relational
All mutual planning done pre-commencement	Post-commencement planning is anticipated
Planning focuses primarily on definition of subject matter of contract	Focus on subject matter but also significant process planning undertaken
Limited *process* planning – and it is mainly directed at dispute resolution	Process planning very detailed and not confined to disputes, but extends to performance, too
Quite likely involves goods of adhesion	Far more mutual planning involved – less likely to involve goods of adhesion
Planning is essentially conflict laden – focuses on 'how much?'	Mixture of enterprise and allocative planning. Former need not be conflictual at all, and latter less conflictual as involves sharing rather than allocation of benefits and burdens

Figure 5.1 The contract planning axis.

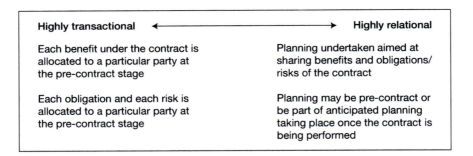

Highly transactional ⟷	Highly relational
Each benefit under the contract is allocated to a particular party at the pre-contract stage	Planning undertaken aimed at sharing benefits and obligations/risks of the contract
Each obligation and each risk is allocated to a particular party at the pre-contract stage	Planning may be pre-contract or be part of anticipated planning taking place once the contract is being performed

Figure 5.2 The incidence of benefits and burdens axis.

Highly transactional ←	→ Highly relational
Source of content is the communicated express agreement of the parties	Source of content is not only original agreement – some at least of the content develops through the relationship and may never be made express
Source of obligation is wholly external (e.g., the courts)	Source of obligation – bindingness arises from sources internal to the parties as well as external sources
Specificity of obligation and sanction is high	Specificity of obligation and sanction likely to be low or even non-existent

Figure 5.3 The obligations undertaken axis.

KEY TERMS

Relationalism

The view that contracts are not one-off, discrete events, but involve sometimes complex and long-term relations, and have a variety of wider contexts in which they need to be viewed to be fully understood.

Relational spectrum

A way of understanding different types of contract according to whether they tend to be close to the paradigm of the transaction or are more highly relational. Contracts will display different features according to where they fall on a transactional – highly relational axis.

Scotch eggs and haggises

Macneil has suggested, rather vividly, that the problem of analysing contracts, and how far one should look at surrounding circumstances, wider economic and social structures and so on, in the case of any individual contract, can be likened to eating a scotch egg inside a haggis. For anyone who does not know: a scotch egg is a hard-boiled egg, surrounded by seasoned sausage meat, and covered in breadcrumbs; a haggis is a Scottish dish consisting of highly seasoned minced sheep's offal, traditionally wrapped in a sheep's stomach, and boiled – it usually has a quite spicy flavour.

He explains that the strong-flavoured haggis will affect the flavour of the sausage meat surrounding the egg, which is already flavoured and will affect the flavour of the egg itself. Thus, the flavour of the egg is affected by the sausage meat first, and then, at another remove, the flavour of the haggis itself, because this affects the flavour of the sausage meat. But, of course, the egg has a flavour of its own, too. In the same way, each contract has special characteristics all of its own, and we can consider it discretely, i.e., separately. Its immediate context (e.g., the industry in question) can have a significant effect on it, and we can, if we wish/need, consider that context. At a further remove, the wider social context may be important and, if it is, we can take that into account. But we will not always and for all purposes need to look at a contract's immediate context (the sausage meat), let alone its wider context (the haggis). It all depends on both the nature of the contract, and on the purposes for which we are analysing it.

The norms of contract

Macneil proposed quite a large number of norms governing contractual relations. These are, he says, 'norms in a positivist sense'.[3] To the legal theorist, this sounds strange. A positivist is someone who believes that the law can be considered in terms of a more or less organised set of 'positive' rules of law. Law students tend to take a positivist approach by default, because they think of law as a system of definite rules governing different types of situation. Textbooks, too, often encourage this approach by trying to set out a definitive statement of a particular area of law, and trying to fit apparently conflicting cases together into a coherent scheme (or else excluding ill-fitting cases as being 'wrongly decided'). Judges also tend to present the law this way in their judgments. What makes the approach distinctively positivist, is that it is an attempt at *description* of what is said to be the case, and eschews viewing the law in terms of what *ought* to be the case, which is called a 'normative' approach.

Macneil explains that he means norms in the sense of 'a pattern or trait taken to be typical in the behaviour of a social group' (quoting from *Websters Seventh New Collegiate Dictionary*). So his norms are 'positivist' because they purport simply to describe what is observably the case, rather than to prescribe what ought to be.

What are they for? Well, it is possible to do various things with a set of norms of this nature, but one of the authors of this book has suggested five main uses:[4]

---

3 I.R. Macneil, *The New Social Contract* (Yale University Press: New Haven, CT, 1980), p.37.
4 See R.L.P. Austen-Baker 'Comprehensive Contract Theory: A Four Norm Model of Contract Relations' (2009) 25 *Journal of Contract Law* 216.

KEY TERMS

Positivism

An approach to any subject that is based on the view that all you can really know of the subject is what is observable. In the legal context, this means cases and legislation from which one can always arrive, somehow, at a single definite rule of law on any point.

Normative

'Establishing a norm or standard' (*SOED*). A normative approach is one based around the idea of what *ought* to be, in the opinion of the person in question, because it sets down what is considered to be proper or 'normal' behaviour.

Normal

'Conforming to . . . a type or standard' (*SOED*).

---

1   They permit the social scientist better to understand and describe economic exchange activity.
2   They enable business people, in designing their relationships with other businesses, better to understand the likely consequences (for the success or failure of their planned relationships) of adopting different alternative approaches to planning those relationships.
3   They allow the drafter of contracts to draft more effectively and efficiently, by enabling the better identification of likely stress points in the relationship in question, and the probable most effective approaches to providing for these.
4   They can assist the judge in discerning what Macaulay called 'the real deal'[5] in commercial disputes and thus to come closer to meeting the real commercial expectations of the parties.
5   They can help the law reformer (e.g., a Law Commissioner, or similar, or a legislator or advisor to legislators or ministers) to ensure that any proposed reform to the legal environment of contract will work with rather than against the needs of real contract relations.

---

5 S. Macaulay, 'The Real and the Paper Deal: Empirical Pictures of Relationships, Complexity and the Urge for Transparent Simple Rules' (2003) 66 MLR 44.

Macneil developed around 14 of these norms (the exact number is really subject to argument):

1 rôle integrity
2 reciprocity (or 'mutuality')
3 implementation of planning
4 effectuation of consent
5 flexibility
6 contractual solidarity
7 the 'linking norms' (restitution, reliance and expectation interests)
8 the power norm (creation and restraint of power)
9 propriety of means
10 harmonisation with the social matrix
11 enhancing discreteness and presentation
12 preservation of the relation
13 harmonisation of relational conflict
14 supra-contract norms.

This list can be gathered together from a number of Macneil's works. To describe what each one means would make this chapter far too long, but you could read Macneil's monograph (an academic book on a particular theme) *The New Social Contract*, which discusses them fully. Austen-Baker has suggested that actually they can be rolled together into just four norms, which he calls 'universal contract norms':[6]

1 preservation of the relationship
2 harmonisation with the social matrix
3 satisfying performance expectations
4 substantial fairness.

Two of these norms have the same names as two of Macneil's norms, but they are slightly different and should not be confused. Let us now look at these four universal contract norms in turn.

Preservation of the relation

Relational contract theories assume that, in most cases, contracting parties are likely to want to keep the relationship going. For most of us, the main contractual relationship we have is our employment – we aim, if we are wise, to earn not less than what we spend, in which case our employment accounts for at least 50 per cent by value of our economic activity.

6 Op. cit., n.4.

Generally, too, this will be a relationship that we will see as being long term and that we will tend to wish to keep going, at least until a better offer comes along.

Other relationships we are in we may not see as being long term or even 'relationships'. While we appreciate that we have long-term relationships with our telephone company, cable television company, broadband provider, bank and so on, which tend to be fairly long term, we probably tend not to think about our relationship with, say a supermarket, in quite the same light. But let us say a family spends an average of £150 a week in its local branch, then the annual spend comes to £7,800 – approaching the purchase price of a brand new small hatchback car every year. A motor dealer would consider a customer who bought a brand new car every year to be rather a good customer and would seek to keep the relationship going. The grocery customer spending £7,800 per annum is probably a reasonably typical, certainly not exceptional, customer for a supermarket chain, but not contemptible for that, and the supermarket is likely to wish to retain the customer's business. (Sir Terry Leahy, then the Chief Executive of Tesco, explained in a Radio 4 programme that he set up Clubcard, the first major supermarket loyalty card scheme, so that he could reward regular custom but, more importantly, to learn about his customers, so he could respond to their changing patterns of shopping and keep them loyal – which perfectly bears out what we have just said.)

There are a good many reasons why contracting parties might want to keep a relationship in being over an extended period. A few examples will suffice to illustrate the breadth of the range of reasons parties have for keeping relationships going:

a   It typically costs more (in terms of average advertising or marketing spend per new customer) to win new customers than to keep existing customers.

b   Transaction costs may be higher outside relations. (i) If replacement business has to be won repeatedly, costs such as carrying out credit checks, setting up accounts, providing initial hardware and installation assistance are also repeated. There will usually be staff time involved in this as well as the supply of hardware. (ii) It is likely that a certain proportion of relations will end in conflict. Such conflict will result in greater costs: lawyers on each side, staff time, diversion of higher management attention, and so on. Multiplying the number of contracts entered into is likely to multiply the absolute number of such conflicts, thereby multiplying the associated costs.

c   A customer might prefer to stay with a particular supplier because it is inconvenient to move (even when it is not very difficult, if people are disinclined or are, to use the current jargon, 'time poor', they may consider it too much trouble all the same), or because they like the service and fear worse service elsewhere.

d   Some contractual relations function better for both sides and become more meaningful as time passes. So, a long-term relationship might serve to make individual transactions under its umbrella more satisfactory for both parties *qua* the transaction itself.

e   Some exchanges depend on trust or work much better in an environment of trust, so that less risk is involved in continuing the relationship (this is true of a good many employment relations, especially, for instance, employing a branch manager of some description, where the employee will have considerable fiduciary responsibilities).

f   Non-economic satisfactions are likely to increase with the longevity of the relationship. Probably all of us are conscious of sometimes making contractual choices based, partly at least, on non-economic satisfaction; for instance, using a particular shop because we have got to know the proprietor or manager and enjoy a little chat when we go in, even though we might get the same goods more cheaply elsewhere.

g   Greater stability is derived from long-term relations than from short-term ones, and planning is easier.

It should be clear that holding relations together is commonly a norm of exchange behaviour. It is suggested that it is so, to some extent, all of the time: contracts are entered into in the expectation of performance, not of breach. Therefore, it is automatically at least a weak norm of virtually all contractual relations, while being a very strong norm in others. A business with a reputation for breaking contracts or for being notable for its involvement in enterprises that fail, is likely to find it at least a little more difficult to do business with those that are aware of this reputation, which indicates that other parties are not generally satisfied with the prospect of a payout from a breached contract: they want, and expect, performance.

The strength of this norm, in any given relation will depend on where the relation in question falls along the transaction–relation spectrum. A number of factors will determine the strength of the norm, as shown in Figure 5.4.

So the norm is stronger in cases where the relation is *expected* to last, rather than to be of short duration. It is stronger where the subject matter is less easily or reliably monetised. The norm is strong where the business sense of the contract depends on the sharing of benefits and burdens over time; weak where there is a clear allocation of defined benefits and burdens at the time the contract is made. Similarly, where measurement of *performance* is easy, so that it can readily be said 'this contract has been performed', exit from the relationship will seem less fraught than where it is harder to determine the completeness of performance. But remember, and note well, that it is the relationship that is sought to be sustained. In traditional contract thinking, each visit to the supermarket involves a separate contract (or several), but it is not meaningful to think in terms of keeping that contract going – once the customer is through the checkout, that is it. It is the *relationship*, the repeat business over a period of time that the supermarket wants to preserve.

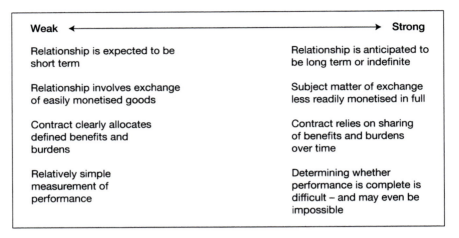

Figure 5.4 Norm of preservation of relationship.

Harmonisation with the social matrix

It is probably best to think of this norm as involving two different ideas: first, that the provisions of the contract rulebook need to be acceptable to the mores of the society in which they are to apply and, second, that individual contractual relations are less likely to survive if they offend against significant local social expectations.

The need for the rulebook to conform to social mores

To what extent do laws reflect, or conflict with, social mores (mores = standards, habits, customs), as opposed to forming them? Let us take the example of exceeding the motorway speed limit as one where people will appreciate that the law needs to set often entirely arbitrary rules in order to prevent excessive and immoral behaviour. Driving in a manner that is thoroughly dangerous and puts other people's lives at risk, perhaps because one is not adequately in control of one's car above a certain speed (a variable according to the skills and condition of the driver, the driving conditions including road width and layout, weather, traffic and, of course, the capabilities of the vehicle), is, no doubt most people would agree, immoral or unethical behaviour. However, while 80 miles an hour on the motorway might be too high for some conditions, cars, and drivers, 100 miles an hour would be perfectly safe for many others. The law, however, draws a very strict and arbitrary line, ignoring these variable factors. The majority of people appreciate these facts and wink at mild infringements, especially where no accident occurs. However, this is far from a universal attitude: there are quite a few people for whom breaking the speed limit is on a par with, say, a mugging or a burglary; that is to say, a crime is a crime and that is all we need to know. For them, the whole question of morality boils down to whether or not something is prohibited by law, in which case, it might be said that law forms morality.

Discussing the extent to which our laws reflect and conform with established social mores is a daily preoccupation of many a politician, jurist and journalist. Every student of contracts can ask him- or herself 'is the rule (or proposed rule) one that could be criticised for being "out of touch", or is it "fit for purpose"?' In doing so, he or she interrogates the rule as to its harmonisation with the social matrix. The uncertainty of the answer is something we have to live with, but the greater the extent to which the questioner is 'in touch', the better.

Still less clear is what the consequences might be of the contract rulebook being out of line with broader social norms. Interestingly, while there have been over the years many debates about laws seen by some (but usually not everyone) to be out of alignment with society at the time – for instance, debates over homosexuality, abortion, vivisection, cloning, research using embryos, gambling – contract law does not seem to have figured. Perhaps, since contract law is an important issue for commerce, changes have always been achieved, whether through occasional legislative intervention or, more often, gradual judicial innovation, with little controversy.

Conformity of individual contract relationships with broader social norms

This question offers perhaps rather less scope for purely academic discussion, but is far more likely to be a pressing practical problem.

One version of the norm of harmonisation with the social matrix is that contractual relations are far more likely to survive and prosper if they are, in as many aspects as possible, in conformity with broader social norms. The more the parties have organised their relationships in such a way that people outside the relationship would consider improper, unethical, immoral, the less likely the it is to survive over a long period or to yield up all the benefits the parties would want to derive from it. Some contractual relationships are, due to their subject matter, automatically regarded as so much at odds with social norms that they are not permitted. The prohibition of some kinds of contractual relationship is explicable in terms of this norm. Others offend against social mores through their processes, and these are doubtfully enforceable. Yet others simply fail to achieve their objectives and, although theoretically enforceable, come to what may be called 'a sticky end'.

Legally prohibited relations

Depending on the contract and the circumstance, legally prohibited contracts can be (1) illegal, (2) void or (3) unenforceable. Treitel identifies three main types of illegality in contracts: 'contracts involving the commission of a legal wrong'; 'contracts contrary to public policy'; and 'contracts in restraint of trade'.

In Treitel's taxonomy of a total of 21 types of contract void for illegality, eight protect what might be called 'the majesty of the law'; that is to say that they strike down what would otherwise be contracts that would undermine the law and its purposes or the courts in which it is dispensed; six protect the sanctity of marriage, love (the reasoning in some cases, at least, being that business arrangements do not accord with proper feelings of marital affection), and family duty; another four protect the interests of the State more narrowly – the State in international relationships, and in its patronage; while the remaining three uphold sexual morality, the liberty of the individual and freedom of trade. Put in these terms, and stripped of the sometimes rather arcane-seeming detail, this is probably – without wishing to undertake an extensive survey of public attitudes – a list of things that most people would agree should be protected and that private contracts ought not to be allowed to undermine. To this extent, they represent a nexus of harmonisation of laws of contract with the social matrix, and this probably is a case of the law being in harmony with broad social attitudes rather than forming them: the details by which the effects are sought to be achieved are surely too abstruse to have caught the popular imagination and thus converted themselves from arbitrary rules to widely held social mores. Here the rulebook conforms and also ensures individual contracts not conforming to these particular norms are weakened by depriving them of official support and even imposing sanctions on the making of them in some cases.

Procedurally compromised relations

In addition to contracts that are (effectively) prohibited by law, some contracts are unenforceable for other reasons that have to do with them offending against social norms. The most egregious examples are where agreement has been obtained by deceit (see *Derry v Peek*)[7] or by duress, whether physical (e.g., *Cumming v Ince*)[8] or economic (see, e.g., *The Atlantic Baron*),[9] or by undue influence (see, e.g., *Royal Bank of Scotland v Etridge (No. 2)*).[10] Other examples are where agreement has resulted from a negligent or innocent misrepresentation, or is the result of a mistake, particularly where the mistake is unilateral so that one party has 'snapped up a bargain' unfairly at the expense of the other (as in *Hartog v Colin & Shields*).[11]

---

  7 (1889) 14 App Cas 337.
  8 (1847) 11 QB 112.
  9 [1979] QB 705.
 10 [2001] UKHL 44.
 11 [1939] 3 All ER 566.

Enforceable contract relations that fail

By 'failure' the present author means that the relation does not survive and prosper long enough or well enough to bring the benefits the parties expected from the relation. One instance of failure would be when the relationship breaks down amid mutual recriminations followed by litigation over a breach of contract. But the contract need not end in breach to be a failure, it merely needs not to succeed in its objectives. (Of course, the objectives may be unrealistic or unreasonable or undesirable, and fail not because of a fault *within* the relation, but rather because the relation was incapable of achieving such ends in any event – say, Accrington Stanley Football Club engaging a man in the pub as its manager, with the intention of winning the European Cup in two years.[12] All sorts of conditions make this an impossible objective, but we do not need any theory of contract to help us understand why that is.)

An example of the latter case might be the Royal Air Force spending millions of pounds on training fighter pilots, who then leave for better money in, say, the Royal Saudi Air Force. The RAF clearly intends that its investment in training will bring the benefit of so much service from a fighter pilot once trained. The relationship has failed when a pilot leaves early to join another air force or become a civilian pilot, even though the pilot has left not in breach of the contract, but terminated it properly in accordance with its terms.

It is at this point that contract theory begins to be interesting to those who are not lawyers or law-makers, because we ask: 'What makes economic relations more or less likely to succeed?' How do we maximise the likelihood of the contract yielding all the benefits we hope and plan for, and minimise the possibility that it breaks down, whether contentiously or otherwise? Relational contract theory in general and Macneil's 'essential contract theory' in particular has tried to answer just this question. The answer, essentially, is that the more the parties ensure that their contract conforms to the norms suggested, the more likely the relationship is to be successful. One aspect of this is that failure is more likely to result if the relationship is not harmonised with broader norms external to the relation.

Examples of the causes of this kind of breakdown are those in which the parties decide not to enter into the relationship at all (not really a failure of a relationship, so much as a failure to enter one; but it is related to what we are discussing here), and those cases in which contracts have to be abandoned because of external disapproval or pressure, aside from purely legal pressures. Imagine, for instance, a hospital's plans to sell off its staff and visitor car parking

---

12 Accrington Stanley FC is an English professional soccer club made famous in a television advertisement for milk in the 1980s in which one small boy tells another that he has been told by a famous soccer player that if he does not drink his milk he will only be good enough to play for Accrington Stanley. The other boy asks 'Accrington Stanley? Who are they?' to which the first replies 'Exactly!' So you could say that it is 'notoriously obscure', which is a neat little paradox.

to a developer of 'executive homes'. The plan may not be illegal in any way and both the parties see advantages. But what happens next? The nurses are out on strike because they have nowhere to park. Doctors are complaining in the press that lives will be put at risk if they have to hunt round for parking places. The local community is up in arms, because it will have nowhere to park when visiting sick relatives in the hospital. The hospital faces a severe public relations problem, and the developer comes in for massive odium throughout the region covered by the local newspapers and television and, quite likely, beyond, if the story makes it into the national media. The plan – seen as one to 'put profits before patients and their families' – is not harmonised with the social matrix, and the parties may well decide that it is not in their joint interests to continue after all, since they cannot clearly balance the unknown future effects of reputational damage and community resentment against the expected short-term economic benefits.

So, the pressures for conformity with broader social norms are both legal and non-legal in origin and both are powerful. Many contractual relationships simply will not come into being if they are too far outside the bounds of social acceptability, others will come under pressure to break down with the mutual assent of the parties, others still might be litigated over because one party attempts to use the non-conformity of the relationship in order to escape from it, perhaps with the benefits.

Satisfying performance expectations

This probably seems somewhat obvious. It is, surely, an expectation that performance expectations will be satisfied. But legal discourse has always entertained doubts about this. In the nineteenth century, Oliver W. Holmes Jr, a Supreme Court Justice and for many years a law professor at Harvard, maintained that the only true obligation in contract was to pay damages for breach. That is to say, there is no obligation to perform stipulated acts (or to refrain, as the case may be) but a conditional obligation to pay damages, which can be avoided by performing as stipulated. Sir Frederick Pollock dismissed this suggestion:

> A man who bespeaks a coat of his tailor will scarcely be persuaded that he is only betting with the tailor that such a coat will not be made and delivered within a certain time. What he wants and means to have is the coat, not an insurance against not having a coat.[13]

The argument persists. At the beginning of the 1960s Harold Havighurst proposed four 'uses' of contract, namely power, peace, enterprise and chance.[14]

---

13 Sir F. Pollock, *Principles of Contract*, 3rd edn (Stevens & Sons: London, 1881), p.xix.
14 See H.C. Havighurst, *The Nature of Private Contract* (Northwestern University Press: Chicago, IL, 1961).

Of these, the first three are, mainly, tied up with the idea of performance. Admittedly, the right to damages is power of a sort over another, but contracts are typically made in anticipation of wider power than this: the power to get something in particular *done*. The peace use of contract cannot be achieved without actual performance (or something like it). Most importantly, the enterprise use is fundamentally *about* performance. It might be argued that enterprise is about getting money, and that damages will do that perfectly well, but that is to look at it from only one person's perspective, namely that of the disappointed innocent party. Society has a need of enterprise, of goods and services being produced, of jobs being created and so forth. The power of contract to enable enterprise depends on contracts being performed. The benefits of enterprise, also, can be seen to go beyond the merely financial and measurable into a wide range of intangible and individual satisfactions, and beyond the individual to wider societal benefits.

Legal scholars often speak of performance of the stipulations of a contract as being performance of the 'primary obligation' and payment of damages as performance of the 'secondary obligation' (e.g., Webb, Friedmann).[15, 16] This is very much against Holmes' view that a contract simply gives a right to choose: do or pay, with the latter on an equal footing with the former.

Implementation of planning

Contracts (insofar as they contain any noticeable degree of futurity) may be said to be 'about' planning. A producer, for instance, with a contract to supply its product to a customer, can purchase raw materials, devote staff time to production, etc., in the knowledge that if the customer refuses to accept and pay for the goods, he will be obliged to pay damages. Thus contract effectuates the implementation of planning. Contract is not, of course, the only projector of exchange, as we have discussed already – non-promissory exchange projectors are at least as important in many activities – but it is an immensely powerful one and a great favourite with enterprise.

Effectuation of consent

Contracts are intimately tangled up with the idea of consent, in that they may be said both to be triggered by consent and to be a mode by which the content of consent may be realised. We agree together on some activity; e.g., the activity of buying and selling a motor car. The consent of one to sell and the other to buy leads to entering the contract: why else? The same consent is typically effectuated by entering a contract; there are other 'hows', of course, but contract is a popular option; indeed, generally in such a case one would need

---

15 C. Webb, 'Performance and Compensation: An Analysis of Contract Damages and Contractual Obligation' (2006) 26 OJLS 41.
16 D. Friedmann, 'The Performance Interest in Contract Damages' (1995) 111 LQR 628.

to take positive steps in order to avoid a contract, in the lawyer's sense,[17] and it is hard to see at all how this is not a contract-*type* relation, even if one were to take such steps. Consent is clearly linked to planning: the planning defines what it is that parties consent to, and parties plan pre-contractually or post-contractually (or, perhaps it is better to say, intra-contractually) for the effectuation of their mutual consent.

What parties tend to be consenting to, of course, is that something be performed. That is to say, that the stipulations of the contract be performed, rather than payment of damages for failure to perform the stipulations. Thus, the notion of the effectuation of consent is tied into the norm of satisfying performance expectations. Taking the example of the householder contracting for work to repair or improve her house, it seems doubtful, at least, that she would consent to enter into a contract with a builder who says frankly at the outset that he does not plan to do the work, but merely to compensate her for the cost of having someone else do it instead, provided she properly mitigates her loss. Our householder wants the work done; that is to say, she only consents to enter into the contract on the understanding that it is intended to cause the stipulated-for primary performance to eventuate. There is no point, as far as she is concerned, entering into the contract merely to become entitled to damages. Would a business do so either? We are inclined to doubt this, too. Some contracts are entered into for specifically financial reasons, for instance insurance, or financial derivatives, but these are quite different as the stipulated-for performance was always intended to be the payment of money on a given contingency. Generally speaking, even businesses contract in order to get things done or delivered, not as a sort of wager, let alone deliberately contracting in vain.[18] The analogy between ordinary contracts and contracts of insurance should not, in short, be taken too far: ordinary commercial contracts are generally entered into to facilitate actual physical enterprise, building cars, for example, not in order to provide insurance against not having components, not having workers, not having a dealer network. One benefit of contract over a 'gentlemen's agreement'[19] is, indeed, that one has some sort of security if

---

17 For instance, declaring any agreement to buy and sell to be 'binding in honour only', see, e.g., *Rose & Frank & Co. v J.R. Crompton & Bros Ltd* [1925] AC 445L.

18 It is true that, in terms of doctrinal contract law, a decision has to be made between whether a court should favour one party's expectation of actual performance or the other party's preference for breaching and paying damages. Ultimately, the latter has been preferred, see especially *Suisse Atlantique Société d'Armement SA v NV Rotterdamsche Kolen Centrale* [1967] 1 AC 361L. But the very fact that such a case as *Suisse Atlantique* reaches the courts, let alone right up to the House of Lords, rather demonstrates the strength of the case for supposing that businesses prefer, and expect, performance, and may place more value on actual performance than on substitutionary awards, a point that has been made time and again in the literature and has led to the coining of the term 'performance interest'. See, e.g., D. Friedmann, *supra*, n.16, and C. Webb, supra, n.15).

19 We mean an agreement intended to be binding, but in honour only – see, e.g., *Rose & Frank & Co. v J.R. Crompton & Bros Ltd*, n.17 above.

the contract is breached, but that is not the sole reason for entering into it. The agreement itself, stripped bare of contractual force, is what is sought, contractual force is added to provide a fallback in damages, and also to disincentivise breach by the other party, because he has less to gain by breaching a contract than by breaching a 'gentlemen's agreement', since in the case of a contract, along with the damage that will accrue from agreement breaking generally (such as the likely inability to deal with that party again in the future, gaining a reputation in the trade for unreliability, and so on) there will be damages to pay as well.

Thus, we may say that the expectation of performance of the express stipulations is the essence of that to which the parties have consented. It is through performance, then, that consent is effectuated in contract.

Creation and restraint of power

One of Macneil's norms is that of the 'creation and restraint of power'. About this he says:

> [T]he very ideas of consent, of contractual planning, of contractual solidarity, and of the linking norms, all presuppose ability to create changes in power relations. When, for example, people sign instalment purchase agreements, they create power in the sellers that they lacked before. Without such shifts of power the other norms would constantly be rendered inoperative. [20]

Various types of power are created by contract, as Macneil goes on to point out:

> Lawyers are most familiar with creation of *legal* power. But power may be economic, social, and political as well; indeed at normal operating levels of contracts, it is those kinds of power, not legal power, that count the most.[21]

Power in contract is also restrained. Macneil finds this exemplified in the 'relatively weak remedies for breach of contract' available in many jurisdictions.[22] This can be seen slightly differently: one person's power created is inevitably another's power restrained. Entering into any contract, we both gain and sacrifice power: we limit our freedom of action within the contract. A weak remedy for breach of contract is not really an example of contract restraining power, since without the contract, there would be less (if any) remedy, thus even less power.

20 *New Social Contract*, p. 56.
21 Ibid.
22 Ibid., p. 57.

So, what is the content of the power? The power may be in nature legal, economic, social, or political, but what is it a power to *do*? Again, the power is one to enforce performance of a promise or else exact a substitute. The law's remedies are relatively weak here, but they restrict the potential gain of the breaching party.[23] The other forms of power, social, economic and political, often provide very strong restraints on the likelihood of refusal to perform. Power (of whatever type) created in contract is both directed at securing stipulated-for performance, and is itself instantiated in that performance.

Rôle integrity

Another aspect of the norm of satisfying performance expectations, which we can discuss here quite briefly, is Macneil's norm of rôle integrity.[24] This idea, for Macneil, comprises three main aspects: consistency, conflict, and complexity. It is submitted that the key aspect is really consistency: consistency over time, and conformity with the rôle. The former refers to the expectation that people will continue (for so long as is relevant in the particular situation) to play a certain rôle.[25] The latter is concerned with what the rôle includes:

> In any given society any particular role is typically not a potpourri of whatever any incumbent wishes to assemble. A role is, among other things, a technique of social control. A limited number of roles will be recognized, and each expected to have some internal harmony. [. . .]
>
> Needless to say, the social limitations on roles need not originate in law or in greater society. Most of them emerge from sources much closer to the workings of the contractual relations themselves. These produce consistency over time as well as a kind of internal consistency resulting both from the specialization and from limited capacities of particular roles.[26]

23 This is presuming one makes the, rather large, assumption that the breaching party really is deliberately breaching in order to make a calculated gain. In the real world of contracts litigation the picture is seldom so clear cut, generally with much argument as to whether acts were in breach and who, indeed, was in breach at any time. Richard Austen-Baker spent long hours in smoke-filled rooms negotiating for one party alleged to be in breach, while in turn alleging the other party is in breach, while himself perfectly convinced that both parties were behaving in all sincerity.

24 *New Social Contract*, pp.40–44.

25 Macneil gives the following example: 'We are all bemused by the cab driver who turns out to be a philosopher, with or without the Ph.D., but bemusement turns to anger if in the middle of the ride from O'Hare Airport he drops us off at a corner with the announcement that he is taking up philosophy full time. His role as a cabbie simply does not permit such a sudden and complete change.' *New Social Contract*, p.41.

26 Ibid., pp.40–41.

Let us ask one simple question here: why does consistency matter? It matters because only insofar as the other party to a relation behaves in conformity with the rôle (e.g., a lawyer we retain is appropriately qualified and expert, keeps our secrets, acts only for us, not our opponent, and otherwise keeps to at least such professional ethics as are relevant to us), and continues in the rôle long enough to perform all the stipulations (e.g., a builder does not decide to become a monk halfway through building our kitchen extension) can our performance expectations be satisfied: this is why rôle integrity is important.

To summarise, the norm of satisfying performance expectations can be taken to include (largely) the functions and contents of Macneil's norms of implementation of planning, effectuation of consent, creation and restraint of power, and rôle integrity. It can also be characterised as being the basis of the 'performance interest' in contracts and offers one theoretical ground for supporting the protection of such an interest in contract remedies.

Substantial fairness

This norm approximately covers the functions of two of Macneil's norms, namely reciprocity (which he originally called 'Mutuality') and propriety of means. Of the first of these, Macneil has written that '[T]he norm of mutuality calls not for equality . . . but for some kind of evenness'[27] and that 'simply stated [it is] the principle of getting something back for something given.'[28] Propriety of means Macneil has defined thus: '[T]he ways relations are carried on as distinct from more substantive matters, including not merely formal and informal procedures, but such things as customary behaviour, often of the most subtle kind.'[29]

One of the present authors (Austen-Baker) has discussed these two norms elsewhere and analysed them in terms of being norms of substantive and procedural fairness, respectively, while also acknowledging that Macneil has distinguished the reciprocity norm (indeed, his norms generally) from 'such less specific, but more familiar, concepts such as good faith, substantive unconscionability, fairness, etc.'.[30] Austen-Baker stands by his approach of treating these norms as being essentially indistinguishable, at least at a working level, from supposedly broader notions such as substantive unconscionability and fairness. We have to work with the vocabulary we have available, the distinctions our language permits, and difficulties arise when we try to differentiate between 'evenness' and 'equality', for instance. The *Shorter Oxford English Dictionary* defines 'evenness' thus: 'The quality or state of being even; smoothness, levelness; uniformity; equability; equipoise (*lit.* and *fig.*); equitableness; equality.'

27 Ibid., p.44.
28 I.R. Macneil 'Whither Contracts?' (1969) 21 *Journal of Legal Education* 403 at 432.
29 Ibid.
30 Letter of 30 April 1998 from Ian R. Macneil to the editors of the *Northwestern University Law Review*.

Evenness, then, can be defined as equality. Equitableness is also in the definition. The *SOED* defines 'equitable' in turn as '[c]haracterized by equity or fairness'. The distinction we have to make is, perhaps, between (as near as possible) perfect fairness and approximate fairness; a notion of something being broadly fair, when all is considered. It is this idea that we are calling here 'substantial fairness'.[31]

Fairness in contract can be considered to embrace both substantive fairness (the 'deal' itself being one that fairly distributes or shares benefits and burdens, not only in its own terms, but, in appropriate cases, also judged in its wider social and economic context), and procedural fairness, being the idea that a contractual relation should be brought about and be conducted in a way that is honest (at least does not cross beyond acceptable bounds of advantage seeking), which, again, may require a contextual approach.[32]

Substantive fairness

As Hugh Collins has pointed out:

> English contract law lacks a general principle of fairness. The courts have set their backs towards such general principles as inequality of bargaining power, a duty to bargain in good faith and testing the adequacy of consideration. [. . .] Instead, the courts rely on particularistic, discrete doctrines, mostly drawn from equity, which can be utilised to counteract patent instances of unfairness.[33]

One example of such a discrete doctrine is the rule against penalties.[34] A number of statutory rules promote (or impose) elements of substantive fairness, for instance, in English statutes, sections 13 and 14 of the Sale of Goods Act 1979, various provisions of the Unfair Contract Terms Act 1977, and elements

---

31 Note 'substantial' not 'substantive', which is, however, a consideration in substantial fairness.

32 For example, what we might regard as sufficiently fair dealing between A and B, we might not consider fair between A and C, where C is a 'vulnerable consumer', say. We recoil (unless we are a tradesperson) from the use of cunning business tactics to 'get one over' on particularly vulnerable people, when we might grudgingly admire it between businesses of similar power. Likewise, what is reasonably acceptable practice in one business, eliciting no more than a shrug of the shoulders, might in another industry be regarded as unethical and result in other firms being reluctant to deal in future with the 'culprit'.

33 H. Collins, 'Fairness in Agreed Remedies', in C. Willet (Ed.), *Aspects of Fairness in Contract* (Blackstone Press: London, 1996), p.100.

34 Originating in the desire to abolish penal bonds: see A.W.B. Simpson, 'Historical Introduction', in M.P. Furmston, *Cheshire, Fifoot & Furmston's Law of Contract*, 16th edn (Oxford University Press: Oxford, 2012). The issue remains a live one raised in the courts today: see, e.g., *Alfred McAlpine Capital Projects Ltd v Tilebox Ltd* [2005] EWHC 281 (TCC), 104 Con LR 39; *Ringrow Pty Ltd v BP Australia Ltd* [2005] HCA 71; *State of Tasmania v Leighton Contractors Pty Ltd* [2005] TASSC 133.

of the Unfair Terms in Consumer Contracts Regulations 1999. Nonetheless, it seems beyond doubt that a norm of substantive fairness is not one that finds powerful protection in the English law of contracts.

Legal force, however, is only one aspect of the power behind contractual norms. A degree of reciprocity, beyond the merely formal reciprocity of the peppercorn rent, has always been needed in economic exchange (at least if not intended as a gift – but even in gifts there can be a hidden reciprocation), so far as we know. In early societies, reciprocity must have been an essential condition of specialisation: without sufficient, substantially fair, reciprocity why would agriculturalists share their produce with the village potter, or the potter supply his wares to the hunter-gatherers? By and large, without sufficient reciprocity in contracts, contracts would not be made at all. What interest would a party have in entering into a contract if nothing was to be gained from it, or the gains were insufficient (as the saying goes, 'the game is not worth the candle')?

In cases where necessity has forced weaker bargainers into contracts in which their commitment is poorly reciprocated, so that they feel that they are getting too many 'harms' to set against the 'goods', social movements respond to the problem. This was precisely the origins of the cooperative movement in England. Shopkeepers were seen to be dealing unfairly with their poorer customers; quality did not reflect price; sharp practices such as adding sand to brown sugar to increase its weight, and thereby cheat the customer, were widespread. The upshot of all this was that first in Rochdale in northern England, then elsewhere, retail cooperatives were established, with fair prices, no sharp practices, surpluses distributed among members (initially these were the staff; later, customers could join the Co-operative Society). It is arguable that late nineteenth- and early twentieth-century retail businesses, such as Sainsbury's, Morrisons, Waitrose and Tesco, could not, against this background, afford to cheat the customer, so that the response of the cooperative movement resulted in forcing greater mutuality, or fairer reciprocation, on private business.[35] Quite apart from such a sectoral effect resulting from a social movement, an individual business that provides relatively poor reciprocation can expect to lose out to its competitors.

By contrast, low quality will often be tolerated quite happily, if the price is also low: people do not usually have unreasonable expectations as to reciprocation; rather, they expect *fair* or *reasonable* reciprocity. Fairness is not

---

35 It might be objected that from 1893 at least, consumers had the protection of the implied terms as to compliance with description and sample, and merchantable quality, but these were unlikely to have meant much or been of any use to the urban working or lower middle classes of Victorian England – the Sale of Goods Act 1893 was framed with what today we call 'business-to-business contracting' in mind, and litigation would have been beyond the means of most people anyway.

an absolute standard of provision or payment, but depends, certainly so far as substantive fairness is concerned, on the quality–price relationship.[36]

It should be borne in mind, while discussing substantial fairness in its aspect of substantive fairness (or adequate reciprocity), that it is not always, or necessarily, the case that price alone fixes expectations as to what is fair reciprocation. A brand may have a reputation for quality at bargain prices. It interferes with quality at its peril, in spite of its competitive prices. The norm of fairness itself makes at least the weak demand that people are not duped into dealing by no-longer true expectations that will now be disappointed;[37] the norm of satisfying performance expectations makes living up to brand or other expectation (irrespective of the objective fairness of relative reciprocity) a very strong demand on contracting parties.[38]

Procedural fairness

The idea of procedural fairness, where the law is mainly concerned with the formation of the contract, including issues such as incorporation of terms, seems to be more strongly protected by the courts. The doctrines of deceit, misrepresentation, all kinds of duress,[39] and undue influence are all ways in which the law of common law jurisdictions (whether common law or equity) approaches the issue of procedural fairness. In a sense, all these doctrines deal with various species of fraud. Contracts the execution of which are procured through duress or the use of undue influence represent a fraud on the law: in such a case the courts are being presented with and asked to enforce what is meant to be a voluntary agreement, but is really nothing of the sort. Deceit

36 Ryanair, the 'no-frills' airline, seems almost to pride itself on its reputation for poor service. But, in this case, poor service, surcharges and the fact that the services are to airports scores of miles away from anywhere most people might want to go to, do not put off too many customers, because such service as they do get is sufficient reciprocation for the extremely low price of the flight tickets (as Ryanair itself frequently points out in response to criticisms of its service in the media).

37 The substantive law would not generally interfere here, so long as price and quality are a reasonable match, but there are areas where the law *does* protect simple expectations based on prior information – that is to say that the law considers it unfair that a party whose expectations have been raised should suffer from a change in circumstances on the other party's side, meaning that s/he will not get the expected performance. Examples of this can be found in the idea of continuing representation (i.e., the duty to speak up if a representation you have made in negotiations that is true when you make it later, but before the contract is concluded becomes false): *With v O'Flanagan* [1936] Ch 575 CA; and in the idea of representation by conduct, e.g., in *Spice Girls Ltd v Aprilia World Service BV* [2002] EWCA Civ 15, [2002] EMLR 27.

38 See the earlier discussion of satisfying performance expectations.

39 Now most importantly economic duress: see, e.g., *North Ocean Shipping Co v Hyundai Construction Co. (The Atlantic Baron)* [1978] 3 All ER 1170; *Pao On v Lau Yiu Long* [1980] AC 614; and *Universe Tankships Inc of Monrovia v International Transport Workers' Federation (The Universe Sentinel)* [1982] 2 All ER 67.

and other forms of misrepresentation (with, in the case of negligent misrepresentation, less degree of culpability, and in the case of innocent misrepresentation, no apparent culpability) involve a species fraud on the other party, who is induced quite voluntarily to enter into a contract he would not have entered into had he known the truth.

Some incidences of operative mistake also involve the taint of procedural unfairness, especially cases of 'snapping up' a bargain, as in the case of *Hartog v Colin & Shields*,[40] in which the plaintiff sought opportunistically to hold the defendant to an apparent bargain to sell hare skins at 10d per pound for 10,000 winter hare skins, 6d per pound for 10,000 half-hare skins, and 5d per pound for 10,000 summer hare skins, whereas the plaintiff knew perfectly well that the defendant's intention had been to offer them for sale at those prices per piece (there being approximately three pieces to the pound for full skins). The plaintiff knew this because it would have been obvious from previous correspondence that these were meant to be prices per piece, and from the trade custom of pricing per piece.[41]

Summary

In brief, it can be argued that where there is substantive or procedural unfairness, going beyond the trivial, then relations will either not occur at all, or will not be sustained (including being sustained by repetition – as with a customer's relationship with a supermarket, for example), and in some cases will not be upheld by a court of law if enforcement is sought. Market forces, including in extreme cases the development of new social movements, will prevent persistent behaviour that is sufficiently widely considered to be unfair, whether substantively or procedurally.

This norm comprehends Macneil's norms of reciprocity and propriety of means, and it also includes an element of the norm of creation and restraint of power, which we dealt with mainly in the discussion of the norm of satisfying performance expectations, since fairness involves giving some powers to parties to enforce fairness in performance, and restraint on the power of the more advantaged bargainer where there is one.

---

40 [1939] 3 All ER 566.
41 There are other examples of this type of case. A case in which it was held that there had been no operative mistake, despite an arguable snapping up of a bargain is *Centrovincial Estates plc v Merchant Investors Assurance Co. Ltd* [1983] Com LR 158 – a decision cited with approval in *Whittaker v Campbell* [1984] QB 318; *The Anticlizo* [1987] 2 Lloyd's Rep 130; and *OT Africa Line Ltd v Vickers plc* [1996] 1 Lloyd's Rep 700, but described by Atiyah as 'absurd and unjustifiable': Sir P.S. Atiyah, *Introduction to the Law of Contract*, 5th edn (Clarendon Press: Oxford, 1995), p.462. Another view might be that *Centrovincial* involved a decision on the facts that it is hard for those not present at the trial to impugn, although in the cold hard prose of the law reports seems an improbable finding.

Practical use of relational theory

There is a fair bit of debate about how the theory should be *used*. It is commonly suggested that we should use the understandings given us by relational theory to help in deciding cases brought before the courts. When judges decline to do this, some academics get rather disappointed, but one might agree with Sarah Bernstein and with Robert Scott that judges should decide cases based on traditional 'rulebook' principles (whether or not one takes as narrow and formalistic a view of those principles as Scott, for instance, does). That does not mean, however, that the theory has no practical value for the lawyer. There are two purposes to which we can apply the theory: analysing existing or anticipated contractual relations and planning new relations. In the case of planning new relations, the ability to analyse the anticipated relationship is clearly of value, so the two purposes are not entirely separate and discrete. Planning a relationship properly is important to making it more likely to succeed in delivering what the parties hope to achieve from it. As the old military adage goes: 'Proper planning prevents piss-poor performance.'

We can analyse a relationship, or proposed relationship, to estimate where on the as-if-discrete to highly-relational spectrum it falls. In many cases we will be able to do this intuitively based on our broad background knowledge of relational theory: a spot oil purchase will be close to the as-if-discrete end, while an indefinite employment contract will lie very close to the highly-relational end. Where it is less obvious at first glance where the relationship falls, we can use some of the axes we looked at early on in this chapter, considering the features or likely features against the descriptions beneath the axes and asking ourselves where, at or between, the extremes this particular aspect or feature of the relation falls. Do that enough times with as many features as possible and we can get quite an accurate picture. We can then use the axes the other way around: placing our relationship at an appropriate point on the axis, we can read down to see what sorts of things we might want to think about incorporating into our planning and the contract which results.

To recap, the axes Macneil drew up are:

1 Overall relationship type.
2 Measurability and actual measurement.
3 Basic sources of socioeconomic support.
4 Duration.
5 Commencement and termination.
6 Planning.
7 Degree of future cooperation required in post-commencement planning and performance.
8 Incidence of benefits and burdens.
9 Obligations undertaken.
10 Transferability.
11 Number of participants.
12 Participant views.

Using these, we can both decide where a particular relation or proposed relation falls and also understand issues affecting our planning. For instance, if using 'overall relationship type', 'measurability' 'duration', 'transferability' and 'number of participants' axes (numbers 1, 2, 4, 10 and 11), we have come to the conclusion that the proposed relation is more towards the highly relational end, we can look at axes 7 and 8 to help us draught a contract that anticipates the need for agreeing some aspects of the deal later, perhaps much later on (with a method of resolving issues where agreement is not reached), which considers a possible scheme for sharing out unexpected gains and losses between the parties, rather than strictly allocating them or letting them lie where they fall. The more axes we use for both the first stage (analysis) and the second stage (drafting), the more complete and perfect our planning, and therefore the performance of the relationship, is likely to be.

Does it have any place at all, though, in litigation? Possibly. An understanding of where the relationship lies on the spectrum, coupled with an examination of axes relevant to the particular contract and the particular dispute, should allow the litigator to understand what the likely expectations of the parties might have been and why some things were dealt with in planning and drafting and others not and to consider, for example, how *reasonable* it might be, in business terms, to contemplate certain matters being dealt with by implied terms and how, indeed, in that event, either party might have responded to the question 'what about a term saying this?': 'of course, it goes without saying' or 'certainly not'. In any event, it never hurts to understand your client and his business better.

Suggested further reading

H. Collins, 'Fairness in Agreed Remedies', in C. Willet (Ed.), *Aspects of Fairness in Contract* (Blackstone Press: London, 1996).

S. Macaulay, 'The Real and the Paper Deal: Empirical Pictures of Relationships, Complexity and the Urge for Transparent Simple Rules' (2003) 66 MLR 44.

I.R. Macneil, *The New Social Contract* (Yale University Press: New Haven, CT, 1980).

I.R. Macneil (Ed., D. Campbell) *The Relational Theory of Contract: Selected Works of Ian Macneil* (Sweet & Maxwell: London, 2001).

I.R. Macneil 'Reflections on Relational Contract Theory after a Neo-classical Seminar', in D. Campbell, H. Collins and J. Wightman (Eds.), *Implicit Dimensions of Contract* (Hart: Oxford, 2003).

6 The economic context of contract law: Part 1

- Economic functions of contract and contract law
- Design of default rules
- Regulation of contractual behaviour
- Standard form contracts
- Contract interpretation

Economic functions of contract and contract law

The economic theories of contract law address questions in relation to efficiency characteristics of contract law. There are two general questions that the law and economics of contract or the economic analysis of contract law aim to answer. The first one is a positive question, namely, is the existing contract law efficient? The second question is a normative one, namely, how can the law of contract be designed to pursue the economic efficiency? To fully appreciate the economic theory of contract law, we should start with the question of what the economic functions of a contract and contract law are.[1]

From an economic perspective, a contract is viewed as a device for resource allocation. Allocative efficiency requires that the resources be allocated to their higher value users. When a change from state A to state B makes at least one person better off and nobody worse off, this change is said to be a Pareto improvement. Compared with other allocative means to allocate resources, such as government action or taxation, contracts have their own advantages. Not only can a contract achieve an efficient allocation of resources, but it can also allocate the resources in a Pareto-improvement way. Suppose in a sale contract, the seller sells his second-hand BMW to the buyer at a price of £10,000. It is reasonable to assume that the seller values the car at less than

---

1 A. Ogus, *Costs and Cautionary Tales Economic Insights for the Law* (Oxford: Hart, 2006), pp.25–31.

£10,000, otherwise he will not sell it for £10,000. For the same reasoning, it is also reasonable to assume that the buyer values the car at more than £10,000. Let us assume that the value of the car to the seller is £9,000 and £11,000 for the buyer. The contract, therefore, moves the car from its lower value user (the seller) to its higher value user (the buyer). This allocation is efficient. More importantly, the allocation makes the both parties better off by £1,000 and nobody worse off. It is a Pareto improvement. The aggregate of their private gains, £2,000, is the social benefit created by the contract.[2]

The primary economic function of contract law is to enforce efficient contracts. Many contracts are instantaneous exchanges in which the parties perform their contractual obligations simultaneously. For instance, a consumer pays cash to buy goods in a supermarket. The consumer fulfils his contractual obligation by paying the price for goods, and at the same time the cashier on behalf of the supermarket performs its part of the contractual obligations by passing on the property in the goods to the consumer. However, there are also many exchanges in which the parties cannot perform their respective obligations simultaneously. They have to do it in sequence. These exchanges are referred to as deferred exchanges.[3] The construction contract is a typical example where one party promises to build a house or another project for the other party first and the payment by the latter party is made on completion of the project. If there were no contract law to enforce agreements, there would be a risk that such an efficient contract would not happen in the first place. As the former party has to invest in the contract in advance, he may be concerned about the risk that the latter party would not keep his promise to pay the money on completion of the project. Contract law provides legal protection for the parties.[4] Where the parties enter into a contract, if one party performs first and the other party refuse to perform his part of the contractual obligations, the law of contract would either force the other party to perform or force him to compensate the former party for his expectation losses from the contract. The law of contract facilitates efficient contracting by enforcing efficient contracts.

The second economic function of contract law is to reduce transaction costs in a contracting process. A transaction cost is often defined in the literature as the expenditure incurred in making a contract, such as effort and money spent on negotiations, costs of drafting contracts, and money paid to the lawyers, etc.[5] Contract law can reduce transaction costs by providing default rules. Higher transaction costs reduce the parties' expected profit from making

2 J. Coleman, 'Efficiency, Exchange, and Auction: Philosophic Aspects of the Economic Approach to Law' (1980) 68 *California Law Review* 221, at 226.

3 A. Dnes, The Economics of Law Property, Contracts and Obligations (London: Thomson, 2005), p.77.

4 R. Cooter and T. Ulen, *Law and Economics*, 5th edn (London: Pearson, 2008), pp.203–207.

5 R. Coase, 'The Problem of Social Cost' (1960) 3 *Journal of Law and Economics* 1.

a contract. If the transaction cost of one party exceeds his expected profit from the contract, he will not be willing to make the contract. Transaction costs impede efficient contracting. Contract law can reduce transaction costs by providing default rules.[6]

A default rule is a legal rule that will become a contract term if the parties do not exclude its application. But if the parties do not like it, they can replace the default rule with their express contract term. Most of the legal rules in contract law are default rules. Taking one of many examples, section 20(1) of the Sale of Goods Act 1979 provides that:

> Unless otherwise agreed, the goods remain at the seller's risk until the property in them is transferred to the buyer, but when the property in them is transferred to the buyer, the goods are at the buyer's risk whether delivery has been made or not.

The phrase 'unless otherwise agreed' indicates that section 20 (1) is a default rule. The parties can replace it by an express term stipulating the transfer of the risk. As we will see later, a default rule can be designed to reduce transaction costs for the parties. If a default rule in contract law is the legal rule that both parties to a contract prefer, they will not spend time and effort on negotiating a contract term to stipulate the issue covered by the default rule. As a consequence, negotiation costs are saved.

The third economic function of contract law is to deter inefficient behaviour in relation to a contract. Although in theory a contract can lead to an efficient allocation of resources in a Pareto improvement way, in practice, there are many contracts that are neither efficient nor a Pareto improvement.[7] The efficiency argument of contracting is based on two very important assumptions. First, it is assumed the individual is rational and the best person to make the decision for himself, and never make incorrect decision. Therefore, whenever he decides to make a contract, the contract must generate benefits for him. The second assumption is that he has perfect information for his decision making. Neither of these assumptions is true in practice. Studies in behavioural law and economics have shown that the human being is bounded and rational and often makes mistakes and wrong decisions.[8] Consequently, the contract that the party made may be an incorrect decision for him. This problem is further exacerbated by the problem of information inadequacy.[9] The party

6 I. Ayres and R.H. Gertner, 'Filling Gaps in Incomplete Contracts: An Economic Theory of Default Rules' (1989) 99(2) *Yale Law Journal* 87.

7 Q. Zhou, 'A Deterrence Perspective on Damages for Fraudulent Misrepresentation' (2007) 19(1) *Journal of Interdisciplinary Economics* 83, at 86–88.

8 C. Jolls, C. Sunstein and R. Thaler, 'A Behavioral Approach to Law and Economics' (1998) 50 *Stanford Law Review* 1471, at 1476–1488.

9 G. Akerlof, 'The Market for 'Lemons': Qualitative Uncertainty and the Market Mechanism' (1970) 84(3) *Quarterly Journal of Economics* 488.

may not always have the adequate information as to his decision making. This may not only lead him to make an incorrect decision but also creates this opportunity for the other party to make fraudulent misrepresentation to mislead him to entering into the contract. The law of contract provides legal remedies for misrepresentation both to compensate the party's losses resulting from the other party's misrepresentation and to deter misrepresentations.

Another inefficient behaviour is to exercise duress or to force the party to make the contract, namely abuse of bargaining power. Where one party is forced to enter into a contract against his will, the contract normally cannot bring him the benefit that he expects to make from the contract. The allocation results from those contracts are inefficient. The law of contract provides legal remedies to regulate the abuse of bargaining power.[10]

The fourth economic function of contract law is to discourage inefficient performance of a contract, or, to put it another way, to encourage efficient breach of a contract.[11] For the parties to a contract, the contract is a device through which to plan their business and to allocate risk. It is quite possible that the basis of a contract may change with the passage of the time. A contract that is viewed as efficient at the time of making the contract may become inefficient later.[12] Such an inefficient contract, from an economic perspective, should be discouraged. Suppose that party A's expectation interest in the contract is worth £100 for him. At the time of contracting, B believes that A can also make a benefit of £100 from the contract. Now B's performance cost increases considerably to £500. If B performs the contract, B will suffer a loss of £400 (£500 − £100 = £400). B's performance is clearly inefficient as A can only benefit by £100 from B's performance, which costs B £500. For the sake of efficiency, B should be allowed to breach the contract and compensate A for his expectation interest of £100. After paying the compensation, A is not made worse off, but B is made better off in comparison of the situation in which B performs the contract because the performance costs him £500 and the compensation only costs him £100. The result is a Pareto improvement. The law of contract can be designed to prevent inefficient breach. We will return to this topic in the next chapter.

Design of default rules

Contract law comprises of two types of legal rule. The first type is the mandatory rule, which the parties must obey as long as they make a contract. The second type is the default rule, which will become a contract term if the parties do not rule it out. But if the parties do not like a default rule, the party

10 Q. Zhou, 'An Economic Perspective on Legal Remedies for Unconscionable Contracts' (2010) 6(1) *European Review of Contract Law* 25.
11 O.W. Holmes, 'The Path of the Law' (1897) 10 *Harvard Law Review* 457, at 462.
12 M. Trebilcock, *The Limits of Freedom of Contract* (Cambridge: Harvard University Press, 1993), pp.19–21.

can exclude it by replacing it with their own express term. In this section, we discuss how to design default rules in contract law. A default rule may fulfil two economic functions. First, it can be designed to reduce transaction costs in contracting and, second, a default rule can also be designed to create an incentive for the parties to share private information.[13]

The function of reducing transaction costs for the parties to a contract is easy to understand. If the lawmaker can provide a default rule that both parties to a contract would prefer to include in their contract, the parties would not need to negotiate such a term, which would save negotiation costs.[14] Of course, in practice, it would be impossible for lawmakers to provide default rules that all the parties to all types of transaction will prefer. Inevitably, a default rule will be preferred by some parties and disliked by others. Transaction costs for society will be minimised by a default rule if the majority of the contracting parties prefer it, because its benefit in terms of saving negotiation costs for the majority of the parties exceeds its cost in terms of the cost of opting out for the minority party. This is called the majoritarian default rule.

Clearly, we should approach this theoretical proposition with a deal of caution. It does not seem easy to design majoritarian default rules in practice. Does the majoritarian default rule exist? The existence of majoritarian default is conditional on the fact that most of the contracting parties have the same preference for the default rules in contract law. This condition requires that all parties to all types of transaction prefer the same default rule, regardless of their differences in industry, transaction and personal expectation from the trade. Obviously, this condition would be very difficult to meet in reality. It is more likely that the parties' preferences are different. For example, a commercial buyer and a consumer buyer often have different views on the best legal remedy for breach of contract. The commercial buyer purchases goods for profit; the consumer buyer does so for personal use. When the seller breaches the contract, the former may prefer the legal remedy that can compensate for the loss of his expected profit, while the latter may prefer one that can provide him with the same goods he purchased. In choosing the default legal remedy, the commercial buyer may favour the remedy of expectation damages, but the consumer buyer may prefer the remedy of replacement. They have different preferences for the default rule. The gap in their preferences will become wider on other important default rules, such as the rules governing pre-contractual duties, passing risk and property.

Furthermore, the parties to a contract are usually in an adversarial position. Most of the legal rules distribute rights and duties between the parties, creating both winners and losers. Often, the legal rule making one party better off

---

13 E. Maskin, 'On the Rationale for Penalty Default Rules' (2006) 33 *Florida State University Law Review* 557, at 558.

14 R. Cooter and T. Ulen, *Law and Economics*, 5th edn (London: Pearson, 2008), pp.217–220.

inevitably makes the other worse off. It is impossible to produce a default rule that both parties will find acceptable. For example, in the sale of goods contract, both parties intend to minimise their personal risk in relation to the goods. The seller wants the risk to pass onto the buyer as quickly as possible, but the buyer wants the exact opposite. The default rule that passes the risk at the time of the formation of the contract makes the seller better off and the buyer worse off. By way of contrast, a default rule that passes the risk over on delivery of the goods makes the buyer better off, but the seller worse off. The parties have conflicting preferences for the default rule in relation to passing over the risk.

If the parties to the same type of transaction do not even have the same preference for the default rule, it is more likely that the preferences of the parties for the different types of contract are much more diverse. It is reasonable to assume that the more varied the transactions, the more disparate the parties' preferences for the default rule, and then it is more unlikely that the majoritarian default rule exists.[15]

Yet, it is by no means the intent here to suggest that the majoritarian default rule never comes into application. In fact, it is more likely to be found where the parties are in the same industry and their private interests have more in common than in conflict. One of such examples is the Uniform Customs and Practice for Documentary Credits (UCP) produced by the International Chamber of Commerce. The latest version is UCP 600, which came into effect on 1 July 2007. The UCP arguably represents the most successful harmonisation of commercial law to date. The law of documentary credit needs to balance three sometimes conflicting interests, namely, the principal who opens the documentary credit, the bank that promises to undertake the payment, and the beneficiary who is assured to receive the payment by the bank. But the major players in drafting the UCP are banks. They have common interests – the codified customs and practice should ensure that banks are not exposed to excessive risks. This is reflected in the whole of the operation of the UCP from the general principle of the autonomy of the credit to specific duties of a bank to exercise due care to check the documents against payment. Unlike the parties to a sale of goods contract, the private interests of individual banks are aligned. They have homogeneous preferences. UCP 600 has been widely adopted by bankers and commercial parties in more than 175 countries, governing financial payments with a total value of more than US$1 trillion every year. The example of the UCP nicely illustrates that when the parties' private interests are in common, the majoritarian preference for the law is more likely to be found; this is a prerequisite for the successful harmonisation of default rules.

---

15 Q. Zhou, 'Harmonisation of European Contract Law: Default and Mandatory Rules', in L. DiMatteo, Q. Zhou, S. Saintier and K. Rowley (Eds.), *Commercial Contract Law Transatlantic Perspectives* 505, at 525–526.

Moreover, the condition that the majority of the contracting parties have the same preference for the default rules is only one prerequisite for the successful design of a majoritarian default rule. Apart from this, the information factor is equally important. Even though the majority of the parties have the same preference, the majoritarian default rule still cannot be produced if the information about their preferences fails to be communicated to the lawmakers.

The amount of information required for this purpose is vast, in particular when the lawmakers intend to produce a single default rule to govern all kinds of transaction.[16] They not only need to find the preferences of the parties to all types of transaction, but also they should be able to generalise the majority preference. This undoubtedly represents a huge challenge for the lawmakers, if not an insurmountable one. This problem is particularly acute in common law jurisdictions where case law is a major source of contract law. A legal rule produced by common law undertakes two stages. First, there must be a dispute between the parties, which is litigated at court, and second, the dispute is solved by judges who will provide legal reasoning both to solve the dispute at hand and to establish the precedent for future judicial decision. There are a number of problems with this procedure of rule making. The fact that parties have a dispute about a contract indicates strongly that the parties do not have the same preference for the term disputed. The judicial decision will inevitably make one party a winner and the other a loser. It cannot be guaranteed that the winner of the dispute represents the preference of the majority of the contracting parties. Even if the decision reflects the majority preference, it is more the result of luck rather than deliberation by the judges. The problem is further exacerbated by the fact that the parties will provide only the information in favour of their own claims. The information presented to judges can sometimes be biased, incomplete, and misleading. Furthermore, the information is related more to the particular dispute at hand. These pieces of information are both imperfect and inappropriate for law making at the general level. They are not representative of general preferences or concerns of the contracting parties to all types of transaction. Generalisation from individual cases is impossible. Finally, when deciding the dispute, judges often do not put themselves in the position of a general lawmaker. Their legal analyses and decisions address the individual case only, although they may consider the impact of this precedent in the future. The effect of this is more supplementary and unintended.

The second economic function of a default rule is to create incentives for the parties to share private information for contract making.[17] Information is crucial for achieving Pareto improvement contracts. Lack of information may

---

16 F. Parisi and V. Fon, *The Economics of Lawmaking* (New York: Oxford University Press, 2009), pp.71–126.

17 A. Kronman, 'Mistake, Disclosure, Information and the Law of Contracts' (1978) 7(1) *Journal of Legal Studies* 1.

cause the parties to make incorrect decisions and enter into an unwanted contract. Nonetheless, the parties may not be willing to share their private information with each other. For example, a commercial buyer often may not disclose to the seller the profits that he will make from the resale of the good. He may be worried that the seller would charge a higher price if he did so.

Another problem facing the parties is unverifiable information. This is a piece of information that cannot be verified by the party at the time of receiving it.[18] There are many products in the market that possess this type of feature. These goods are often called experience goods (e.g., a holiday, education or books). A buyer cannot judge the quality of a book when purchasing it. He can only judge its quality after reading it. By that time it will be too late if the book is of poor quality. This type of information problem in its most severe form may give rise to the notorious calamity in the market, namely the problem of a 'market for lemons'.[19]

Suppose that there two types of author who write romantic novels, namely, a good author and a bad author. It costs the good author £10 per copy to write a high-quality novel, but only £5 for a bad author to write a low-quality novel. When purchasing a book, readers cannot distinguish the good books from the bad. Rational readers will factor the uncertainty over the quality of the book into the price that they are willing to pay for it. Assume further that a rational reader believes that he has a 50 per cent chance of purchasing a bad book. He is only willing to pay £7.50 (£10 × 50% + £5 × 50% = £7.50) for a book when he cannot judge its quality at the time of buying it. However, at the price of £7.50 per copy, the good author is unable to recover the cost of writing a high-quality novel. He is left with two options: either to write low-quality novels only, as these cost him £5 per copy, or to quit the market. Following this reasoning, the only goods sold in the market will be those of the lowest quality. The market becomes a 'market for lemons'.

There are many regulatory laws that impose a mandatory duty of information disclosure on the parties to given transactions, such as listed companies, traders of goods and other consumer products.[20] Alternatively, contract law can use the default rule to create an incentive for the parties to share their private information.

This means can be used jointly with the mandatory duty of information disclosure or as its alternative. In pursuing this purpose, a default rule should be designed as a legal rule that disadvantages the party who has private information so that he will replace the default rule with an express term. By

---

18 A. Ogus, *Regulation: Legal Form and Economic Theory* (Oxford: Hart Publishing, 2004), pp.38–41.
19 G. Akerlof, 'The Market for 'Lemons': Qualitative Uncertainty and the Market Mechanism' (1970) 84(3) *Quarterly Journal of Economics* 488.
20 A. Ogus, *Regulation: Legal Form and Economic Theory* (Oxford: Hart Publishing, 2004), pp.121–50.

doing so, the law also induces him to disclose his private information to the other party. There are many default rules in contract law fulfilling this function. The typical example of this kind is the doctrine of remoteness in the calculation of damages for breach of a contract. As a general principle, a party is unable to recover the loss as result of the other party's breach, if such losses could not be unforeseen or should have been reasonably foreseen by the parties at the time of making the contract. In English contract law, the doctrine of remoteness was established in the case of *Hadley v Baxendale* (1854) 9 Exch 341. The claimant was a mill owner. He entered into a contract with the defendant, a carrier. They agreed that the defendant would carry a broken crankshaft from the claimant's mill to a third-party engineer in London for repair and then deliver it back after the repair. The defendant breached the contract by delaying in the delivery of the crankshaft to the engineer. This caused a complete loss of production at the mill for five extra days. What was unknown to the defendant at the time of contracting was that the claimant had reached a very profitable deal with another party. The defendant's delay caused the claimant to lose this profit in this 'secret business'. The claimant sought to recover his profit losses. The court ruled that the claimant was only entitled to recover the normal profit, but was not entitled to recover the profit in the 'secret business' because this deal was either unknown to the defendant, or should have been foreseen by the defendant at the time of contracting. It is often said that the doctrine of remoteness in English contract law has two limbs. First, damages for breach of a contract is recoverable to the extent to which the loss is considered fairly and reasonably to arise naturally from such a breach; and, second, the loss is reasonably supposed to have been in the contemplation of both parties at the time they made the contract as the probable result of the breach.

The doctrine of remoteness encourages the parties to disclose their private information as to their contract performance value. It limits the recoverable damages to the extent of normal profit in the given business. Obviously, the party that has a higher value in contract performance does not prefer this rule. He will then make the other party aware of his high subjective value in the performance. The underlying reasoning is simple. By designing the default rule in a way that disadvantages the party that possesses the private information if he does not disclose it, the law creates an incentive for the party to disclose information.[21]

Another example for designing the default rule in this way is the doctrine of frustration, which releases the parties from contractual obligations when the fundamental purpose of the contract cannot be achieved because of an unforeseeable event that is no fault of either party. From an economic

---

21 G.S. Geis, 'Empirically Assessing Hardley v. Baxendale' (2005) 33 *Florida State University of Law Review* 879.

perspective, the doctrine of frustration is a default allocation of risk. When it operates, it allocates the risk of the unforeseeable event to the party that is entitled to contract performance by releasing the party owing the contractual obligations. Following the reasoning discussed earlier, scholars of law and economics suggest that the doctrine of frustration is inapplicable when the party owing the contractual obligation can avoid or insure the risk at a lower cost in comparison to the other party. By doing so, the doctrine of frustration creates an incentive for the party that can manage the risk at the lowest cost to manage the risk.[22] The result is economically efficient. In brief, a default rule can be designed to create an incentive for the disclosure of private information by making the rule disadvantage the party with the private information. Consequently, the party is induced to replace the default rule with an express term, and private information is also disclosed accordingly.

Nonetheless, this process has a number of limitations and does not always work effectively. It assumes that the parties are aware of the default rule and then are able to respond to it accordingly. This is not always true in reality. The default rule will have no effect on the parties if they are not aware of it or, even if they are aware of it, they fail to appreciate its legal effects. In addition, another problem is that even if the parties fully appreciate the default rule, they are unable to produce a proper express term to replace it. Take the doctrine of frustration as an illustration. Following the economic reasoning, the doctrine should be used to induce the party that could incur a lower cost to avoid, manage or insurance the risk to manage the risk. It should not release the party's contractual obligations if he is considered the 'least cost avoider' of the risk. This requires the judge to use counterfactual analysis to evaluate the case at the time of contracting. The judge may err in his evaluation by making the incorrect decision. It is also possible that the party who is perceived as the 'least cost avoider' did not contemplate the risk and therefore was unable to manage it, because the risk was unforeseeable to the party. In the famous English case on the doctrine of frustration, *Krell v Henry* ([1903] 2 KB 740), the defendant hired the claimant's flat for two days to view King Edward VII's coronation. Unfortunately, the king was ill and the ceremony was cancelled. The court held that the contract was frustrated and both parties were released from their contractual obligations. The operation of the doctrine of frustration in this case literally allocated the risk of cancellation of the ceremony to the landlord claimant by releasing the defendant's obligation to pay the rent. It seems to be that the economic reasoning is hard to apply to this case. On the one hand, it is very hard to judge who is the least cost avoider between the landlord claimant and the tenant defendant; on the other hand, it is reasonable to say that the risk was unforeseeable to both parties.

---

22 R. Posner and A. Rosenfield, 'Impossibility and Related Doctrines in Contract Law: An Economic Analysis' (1977) 6 *Journal of Legal Studies* 83; G. Wagner, 'In Defense of the Impossibility Defense' (1995) 27 *Loyola University of Chicago Law Journal* 55.

One might argue that the event was foreseeable as it is not too hard for the parties to contemplate the risk that the king might be ill. However, even if the risk were foreseeable, how could the parties manage the risk *ex ante*? Presumably, the parties may have a contract clause to deal with the risk. But this incurs additional negotiation cost. It is hard to say if the additional cost is justified given the likelihood of the risk.

Finally, even though a default rule can be designed to induce the party to disclose his private information, it is not always efficient to do so. To be efficient, the cost of the default rule must be the lowest in comparison with other alternative rules. Take the doctrine of remoteness as an example. According to the legal rule established in *Hadly v Baxendale*, the party that has a higher value in the performance is unable to recover the part of his loss that exceeds the normal performance value in the market. It encourages the high-value party to disclose his subjective value by writing an express term to replace this default rule. Writing an express term is costly. From the standpoint of the society as a whole, the rule in *Hadly v Baxendale* is only efficient if the majority of the contracting parties in the market hold a normal performance value and only the minority of them have a higher performance value. Otherwise, the cost of excluding the doctrine of remoteness will exceed its benefit in terms of saving transaction costs. Empirical studies have shown that the default rule of remoteness is more efficient in simple markets in which transactions share same or similar conditions, but is inefficient in markets in which transactions are heterogeneous and most of the parties hold a high performance value.[23]

Regulation of contractual behaviour

From a perspective of the conventional legal wisdom, the law of contract fulfils a facilitative rather than a regulatory function. In other words, the majority of legal rules in contract law are default rules and rarely are there mandatory rules. Nonetheless, in a number of cases, the law of contract does perform a regulatory function in policing contract behaviour. Some forms of contracting behaviour are inefficient to society and lead to a misallocation of resources such as fraudulent misrepresentation, duress and undue influence. All these conducts share a same feature in that they induce one party to make a contract that he would not have made had he not been induced. As a consequence, not only would the contract not be a Pareto-efficient allocation of resource, but also would generate a social cost. Take fraudulent misrepresentation as an example. The seller induces the buyer to purchase his car for £1,000 by exaggerating the quality. Had the seller told the truth, the buyer would only have been willing to pay £500 at most for the car. Apparently, this transaction would not be Pareto improvement allocation of the car. The seller's

---

23 G.S. Geis, 'Empirically Assessing Hardley v. Baxendale' (2005) 33 *Florida State University of Law Review* 879.

misrepresentation generates a £500 loss to the buyer and £500 gain to the seller. From an efficiency standpoint, there is neither social loss nor gain. It is merely a transfer of wealth from the buyer to the seller. A fraudulent misrepresentation and other forms of exploitative contracting behaviour are undesirable, not because they cause a transfer of the wealth from one party to the other, but because they generate real social costs. There costs fall into three categories, namely, the cost of misallocation, precautionary cost and the cost of undertaking exploitative contracting behaviour.[24]

From an economic perspective, an exploitative contracting behaviour causes a misallocation of resources by misleading people into making an incorrect decision, which will result in social welfare losses. For example, where there are many misrepresentations that exaggerate the quality of the goods, some buyers would be misled into purchasing goods at a price that they would not have been willing to pay had they known the truth. From society's standpoint, this would cause an excessive supply of goods than the optimal level. This would be a social welfare loss. Second, exploitative behaviour generates precautionary costs, which can be defined as the money effort and time used by the contracting party to prevent exploitative behaviour. If exploitative behaviour cannot be entirely eliminated, market participants have to take precautions to prevent being exploited. For instance, the contracting party may devote more time and effort to searching for the relevant information to prevent being misled by misrepresentation. This is a social cost to society, because it can be invested in a more efficient alternative use. The third type of social cost generated by an exploitative behaviour is the cost of undertaking such a behaviour. An exploitative behaviour is a form of opportunistic behaviour. The resources devoted to this kind of behaviour are dissipated because it does not increase social welfare, but merely transfers existing wealth between the parties. Therefore, the more parties there are investing in exploitative contracting behaviour to capture a bigger share of contract surplus, the less surplus will remain. The resource used in this way is totally wasted from the perspective of society as a whole.

Despite this imperfection, the law of contract does perform a regulatory function to deter exploitative contracting behaviour by using the remedy of damages or rescission. The traditional economic analysis of individual behaviour sees it as the result of a cost–benefit calculation. It is assumed that the person will assess the expected costs and benefits of a proposed act and will decide whether or not to proceed on the basis of this balancing approach. A legal remedy is then simply seen as an instrument by which the cost of the behaviour for the person can be increased. Thus, to deter a person from behaving in a certain way, the law could use a legal remedy to increase the cost to him of that behaviour, so that he could no longer profit from so

---

24 Q. Zhou, 'A Deterrence Perspective on Damages for Fraudulent Misrepresentation' (2007) 19(1) *Journal of Interdisciplinary Economics* 83, at 86–88.

doing.[25] Based on this theory, we could create a deterrence model of legal remedy for unconscionable contract: $Dq > G$

Here, D presents the private legal remedy for unconscionable contract; q stands for the probability of private legal enforcement. In reality, the enforcement is imperfect, so, $q < 1$, but > 0. G is the contracting party's profit from writing the unconscionable term. If this inequality is held, the party will be unable to make a profit from writing the unconscionable term. Therefore, the remedy creates an effective deterrence. Now let us apply this model to the analysis of the legal remedies for exploitative contracting behaviour, viz., damages and rescission.

The remedy of damages can be defined as a sum of financial compensation paid by the wrongdoer to the victim of his wrongdoing. Compared with the remedy of rescission, the deterrence of damages is more effective. In theory, such deterrence will always be effective, even if the legal enforcement of a private law remedy is imperfect, as is normally the case in reality. This is because there is no upper limit for setting the level of damages, D. If the probability of legal enforcement is imperfect ($q < 1$), D can always be increased to achieve $Dq > G$ by setting

$$D \geq \frac{G}{q}.$$

To illustrate, suppose that the seller could make a profit of £100 from including an unfair term in the contract, viz., G=£100, and that legal enforcement is perfect, $q = 1$. The law could effectively overcome the party's incentive to include the unconscionable term by setting damages at £100, thereby eliminating the profit from the unconscionable term. If the legal enforcement is imperfect, $q < 1$, the effective deterrence can only be achieved by setting D higher than the profit, so that

$$D \geq \frac{G}{q}.$$

For example, let us assume that $q = 0.85$. After D is discounted by q, Dq is £85 ($0.85 \times 100 = 85$), which is less than G, £100. This indicates that the seller can still make a net profit of £15 after being sanctioned by damages. To create an effective deterrence, D ought to be increased to at least £117. Only this way can the seller's net profit be reduced to nil.[26] This analysis has two implications. First, there are two ways to enhance deterrence: we could

---

25 Q. Zhou, 'A Deterrence Perspective on Damages for Fraudulent Misrepresentation', *Journal of Interdisciplinary Economics*, 19 (2007), 83–96, at 88; G. Becker, *The Economic Approach to Human Behaviour*, 1st edn (University of Chicago Press: Chicago, IL, 1976).

26 If $q = 0.85$, and G = 100, G/q = 117, so D should be set at 117.

either increase the level of legal sanction, D, or improve the legal enforcement, q. When both strategies are plausible, we should choose the one with the lower administrative cost. Second, in the case of imperfect legal enforcement $(0 < q < 1)$, damages can always be adjusted to achieve effective deterrence by setting

$$D \geq \frac{G}{q},$$

because there is no upper limit for the level of D. As will be seen later, the remedy of rescission has an upper limit for D, which therefore cannot be set in excess of this limit to achieve effective deterrence in the case of imperfect legal enforcement.

Another remedy for an exploitative behaviour is the right to rescission. Where one party is induced to a contract by the other party's exploitative behaviour, the contract is voidable. The aggrieved party can rescind the contract. The parties should return to each other the value that they received form the other party. The contract is brought back to the position in which no contract had been formed. This is a radical contract law remedy. Declaring a contract void *ab initio* not only poses the danger of uncertainty in the law, but also confers a considerable judicial power on courts.[27] Compared to the remedy of damages, the deterrence of rescission is less effective. Three remarks should be noted.

First, if legal enforcement were perfect $(q = 1)$, the remedy of rescission would create the same degree of deterrence as damages. Once the contract is rescinded, neither party can realise its expected interest from the contract. Therefore, D, the liability cost to the party under the remedy of rescission, equals his expected profit from the exploitative behaviour, which is measured as his expected profit from the transaction and the extra profit brought by the exploitative behaviour, G. Therefore, the deterrence of invalidation of contract is effective, because if $q = 1$ and $D > G$, Dq always exceeds G.

Second, the deterrence of rescission is still effective in the case of imperfect legal enforcement $(q < 1)$, if

$$q \geq \frac{G}{D}.[28]$$

This implies that as long as the reduction in the probability of legal enforcement is not less than the ratio of the overreaching party's expected profits from the exploitative behaviour to the expected profit from the contract, the deterrence is still effective.

27 B. Markesinis, H. Unberath and A. Johnston, *The German Law of Contract: A Comparative Treatise*, 2nd edn (Oxford University Press, Oxford, 2006), p.248.

28 Q. Zhou, 'A Deterrence Perspective on Damages for Fraudulent Misrepresentation', *Journal of Interdisciplinary Economics*, 19 (2007) 83-96, at 88.

Third, if

$$q < \frac{G}{D},$$

the deterrence of rescission is ineffective and the deterrence can be enhanced only by improving the legal enforcement, q. Unlike the remedy of damages, under the remedy of rescission D is fixed: it equals the party's expected profit from the contract. Therefore, the deterrence cannot be improved by increasing D. This is why, in terms of deterrence, damages are a preferable remedial alternative to the remedy of rescission, when legal enforcement is poor.

Standard form contracts

Standard form contracts are also called 'boilerplate' or adhesion contracts in the American legal literature, and have been widely used in both commercial and consumer transactions. A standard form contract is drafted by one party; the other party often cannot negotiate on the terms and only has the options to accept or reject the whole contract. Sometimes, a standard form contract is drafted by a third party such as a trade representative or association. One major criticism of the standard form contract in the conventional legal literature is that it violates the theoretical foundation of a contract, namely freedom of contract.[29] There is one party at least to the contract who is unable to negotiate on the terms. This gives rise to a risk that the stronger party may exploit the weak party by drafting a standard form contract in his own favour.[30] Where the stronger party does not have competitors in the market, the weaker party will be forced into accepting an unfair standard form contract. The standard form contract is not concluded on the basis of freedom of contract.

From an economic perspective, standard form contracts have three obvious benefits. First, standard form contracts can reduce transaction costs. In the case of a standard form contract, the party receiving the contract only has the option to accept it or reject it as a whole. There is no option for further negotiation on the terms. Accordingly transaction costs are saved.[31] However, the key question is if the absence of negotiation is ultimately efficient to society. The outcome is uncertain. The stronger party may exploit the weaker party by the standard form contract; on the other hand, the party drafting the contract may also provide the terms that both parties would have been willing to accept. In the latter case, the standard form contract is socially

29 A. Leff, 'Contract as Thing' (1970) 19 *American University Law Review* 131–157.
30 R. Korobkin, 'Bounded Rationality, Standard Form Contracts, and Unconscionability' (2003) 70 *University of Chicago Law Review* 1203.
31 C. Gillette, 'Standard Form Contracts', in G. Geest (Ed.), *Contract Law and Economics* (Cheltenham: Edward Elgar, 2011), p.115.

efficient even though it is absent of negotiation by the parties. The key law-and-economics question is how the legal rule is designed to facilitate drafting of efficient standard form contracts and at the same time to prevent misusing standard form contracts. Empirical evidence shows that efficient standard form contracts are more likely to evolve from repeated transactions between sophisticated contracting parties.

Second, standard form contracts may realise the benefit of network externality.[32] One of the thorny problems with contract law is certainty over the interpretation of a contract. Standard form contracts may mitigate this problem. Where a given version of a standard form contract is repeatedly used in the market, the parties will gradually be led to an agreement on the meaning of the terms. when a dispute on a particular term in the standard form contract reaches to the court, the judicial interpretation of the term becomes public and learnt by all of the players using the standard form contract in the market. In the long term, vague terms and uncertain interpretations of the standard form contract will disappear. In other words, standardisation of contracts reduces uncertainty over vague contract terms by inducing all players (both contracting parties and judges) to come to an agreement on the meaning of the contract terms.

Third, standard form contracts may abate the agency problem in mass transactions.[33] In many modern transactions, agents are used as an intermediary to distribute products by manufacturers or wholesalers to end users, retailors and consumers. If the principal authorises the agent to negotiate the terms of a contract, the principal has to monitor the agent to ensure that the agent does not pursue his or her own self-interests at their expense. To raise his commission, the agent may agree terms with a third party that are very onerous to the principal. Without proper control of the agent, the principal is exposed to unjustifiable and inefficient risks that the agent undertakes on his behalf. Standard form contracts mitigate this problem by preventing the agent from changing the terms in the contract. As a result, agency costs are reduced.

Despite the merits noted here, standard form contracts also give rise to certain problems that justify the regulatory intervention. Proponents of standard form contracts argue that, in a competitive market, standard form contracts are efficient because competition will drive firms to provide efficient terms, otherwise consumers will switch to their competitors. In reality, a perfect competitive market has never existed. In many industries, such as utility sectors, mobile phone and internet markets, and insurance sectors the market is far from perfectly competitive. Consumers in those markets do not have

---

32 Ibid. at p.116.
33 Ibid.

sufficient choice in alternative providers. Often the service providers offer more or less the same standard form contract. It is not warranted that the market drives firms to offer the same efficient standard form contract; it is quite possible that the firms have oligopoly power and provide consumers with the same inefficient contracts. Consumers have no alternative but to accept the onerous contract. It is certainly cannot be assumed that the wide use of standard form contracts is a result of competition in the market and this, therefore makes it efficient. It may be evidence of imperfect competition in the market that needs regulatory invention.[34]

The pervasive use of standard form contracts may obstruct contractual innovation. The network effect of standard form contracts leads the parties to use the same standard form contract. As the standard form is used by many or all of the contracting parties in the market, it creates a problem for positive externality. More and more parties will use the existing standard form contract, but fewer parties will be willing to draft a new standard form contract. In the long run, the existing standard form contract will become obsolete and inefficient. The supply of standard form contract in the given sector is lower than the optimal level.

Furthermore, studies in behavioural law and economics also vividly illustrate the problems with the wide use of standard form contracts. Empirical studies show that consumers neither have sufficient information and knowledge to understand some terms in standard form contracts nor do they make a great effort to read the forms through. Consumers are sometimes vigilant about certain contract terms such as price and quality, but are less so when it comes to other important terms such as jurisdiction clauses, applicable law clauses and exclusion clauses. There is an ample opportunity for firms to exploit consumers by drafting standard form contracts. For example, firms may conceal certain information as to 'add-on' costs from consumers thereby inducing consumers to purchase their products. A seller of printers may charge a lower price for the printer itself, but does not disclose that the printer must use the unique cartridge produced by the same company and overprices cartridges. Less sophisticated consumers may be misled into purchasing, only the printer realising later that they have to buy overpriced cartridges.

Contract interpretation

Contractual interpretation is the judicial activity in which the judge is asked by the parties to a contract to articulate the meaning of a term in the contract. In a dispute on the contractual interpretation, the parties have a different understanding of the meaning of a term in the contract that they agreed. When such a dispute arises, the judge is required to provide a judicial interpretation

---

34 O. Bar-Gill, *Seduction by Contract Law, Economics and Psychology in Consumer Markets* (Oxford: Oxford University Press, 2012), chs 2–4.

of the disputed term. For example, in *Mid Essex Hospital Services NHS Trust v Compass Group UK and Ireland Ltd (t/a Medirest)*,[35] the appellant and the respondent agreed that the respondent would provide catering and cleaning services for two hospitals in Essex. Clause 3.5 provided:

> [The appellant and the respondent] will co-operate with each other in good faith and will take all reasonable action as is necessary for the efficient transmission of information and instruction and to enable the [appellant] or, as the case may be, any Beneficiary to derive the full benefit of the Contract.[36]

The dispute was on the interpretation of good faith in this clause. The respondent argued that Clause 3.5 should be read as if it had the following punctuation and numeration:

> The [appellant and the respondent]:
> (1) will co-operate with each other in good faith; and
> (2) will take all reasonable action as necessary:
>   (a) for the efficient transmission of information and instructions; and
>   (b) to enable the [appellant] or, as the case may be, any Beneficiary to derive the full benefit of the Contract.[37]

According to this reading, the parties owed each other a general duty of good faith. The appellant presented an alternative reading of the clause:

> The [appellant] and the [respondent] will co-operate with each other in good faith and will take all reasonable action as is necessary:
> (1) for the efficient transmission of information and instruction; and
> (2) to enable the appellant or, as the case may be, any beneficiary to derive the full benefit of the Contract.[38]

According to this latter version, the duty of good faith should be restricted to the purposes of (1) and (2) only. The court is required to choose one of them.

There are three major approaches to the contractual interpretation, namely, the literal approach, the contextual approach and the doctrine of *contra proferentum*. The literal approach to the contractual interpretation requires the judge to construe the term according to the ordinary grammatical meaning of the words.[39] The approach prohibits the party assigning to the term a

---

35 [2013] EWCA Civ. 200.
36 Ibid., at [14].
37 Ibid., at [97].
38 Ibid., at [98].
39 Lovell & Christmas Ltd v Wall (1911) 104 LT 85.

meaning that a reasonable person who is competent in English cannot articulate by reading the term. The extrinsic evidence ought not to be admitted for the purpose of the interpretation. In contrast, the contextual approach requires the judge to consider relevant extrinsic materials rather than the text itself when construing the term.[40] The doctrine of *contra proferentem* is used in the interpretation of a standard form contract or an exclusion clause. According to this doctrine, where an ambiguity arises, the judge should interpret the ambiguous term against the party who drafts the contract.

The key economic question as to the contractual interpretation is to minimise two types of transaction cost. The first type of cost is the cost of drafting a more complete and detailed contract. The second type of cost is the judicial cost, which includes both the economic costs spent on the interpretation of the term by the judge and the error cost.[41] The judicial cost only occurs when a litigation arises. It is reasonable to assume there is an inverse collation between the two types of cost. The more complete and detailed the contract is, the lower the possibility that the party will have a dispute on the understanding of the contractual term, and the lower the cost of judicial interpretation. A simple model may help readers to understand the economic implications.[42] Let C stand for the total social cost, x represents the parties' cost of negotiation and drafting, p is the probability of litigation, y is the cost of judicial interpretation, and e is the error cost. Then we can develop the following model: $C = x + p(x) \cdot [y + e]$

The first term on the right-hand side of the equation, x, stands for the first stage of ascertaining the meaning of the term. At this stage, it is the contracting parties who decide the degree of precision of the term. The more precise the term is, the higher the value of x. The second term on the right represents the second stage of determining the meaning of the term when the parties have a disagreement on the contract and the litigation arises. At this stage, it is the judge who construes the meaning of the term. The economic goal of designing the legal principle of contract interpretation is to minimise the total cost, C, by inducing the parties to invest the optimal level of x. The value of C differs in the three types of approach to the contractual interpretation.

The literal approach generates a higher drafting cost, but a relatively lower judicial cost. It does not need the judge to consider extrinsic evidence. In comparison with the contextual approach, the judge invests a lower effort in the interpretation and the probability that the judge construes the term in conflict with the meaning which the parties agreed at the time of making the

---

40 C. Mitchell, *Interpretation of Contract* (London: Routledge, 2007), p.4; *Investors Compensation Scheme Ltd v West Bromwich Building Society* [1998] 1 WLR 896, 912–913.

41 The error cost is defined as the cost resulting from the judge's incorrect interpretation of the term.

42 This model is based on Posner's economic model of contract interpretation, see R. Posner, 'The Law and Economics of Contract Interpretation' (2005) 83 *Texas Law Review* 1581 at 1583.

contract is lower. Therefore, the sum of y and e is lower too. However, this approach increases the drafting cost to the parties. As the judge does not consider the extrinsic evidence, the literal approach creates the incentive for the parties to draft the contract with great detail and precision. Consequently, the value of x is high.

From an economic perspective, the literal approach to the contractual interpretation is likely to be efficient when the parties have more information advantages so that the cost of drafting is lower than the judicial cost. In addition, the parties' bargaining positions are relatively equal. Otherwise, the contract is drafted predominantly by one party; the other party does not have leverage to negotiate on the terms. The literal approach may undermine the freedom of the contract, by unduly favouring the dominant party. Thus, this approach is more suitable for commercial contracts than consumer contracts.

The contextual approach generates a higher judicial cost and a lower drafting cost, as this approach allows the judge to consider materials other than the text itself in construing the contract. The judge will put more effort in the interpretation; accordingly, the chance that he may provide an incorrect interpretation is also higher. But this approach creates less incentive for the parties to draft a detailed and precise contract. They may rely more on the judge's construction of the contract if there is dispute on the meaning of a term. This approach is more likely to be efficient when the factor of information is not of great importance for the interpretation of the contract. For example, where there has been a set of trade usages that have been adopted widely in the industry, it is not difficult for the judge to ascertain the meaning of a given usage. In this case, there would be no need for the parties to write a detailed contract, but incorporate the usage into the contract. The context approach is efficient by saving the parties' drafting costs. At the same time, the judicial cost is not very high because not only it is not difficult for the judge to ascertain the meaning of a particular trade usage, but also the judicial cost only incurs when the litigation arises. If the parties do not have a dispute about the meaning of the contract, the judicial cost is saved as well.

Similar to the literal approach, the doctrine of *contra proferentum* also generates a higher drafting cost and a lower judicial cost. But there is a key difference between the two approaches. The literal approach increases the drafting cost for both parties. By way of contrast, the doctrine of *contra proferentum* only increases the cost for one party, normally the dominant party who drafts the standard form contract or exclusion clauses. As this doctrine requires the judge to interpret the term against the party who drafts it, it creates not only the incentive for the party to draft a clear contract, but also an incentive to draft a fair term. This doctrine is more likely to be efficient in consumer contracts where the consumers do not have leverage or chance to negotiate with the traders. It can balance the parties' bargaining leverage and regulate the abuse of bargaining power.

Suggested further reading

I. Ayres, and G.H. Gertner, 'Filling Gaps in Incomplete Contracts: An Economic Theory of Default Rules' (1989) 99(2) *Yale Law Journal* 87.

O. Ben-Shahar, 'A Bargaining Power Theory of Default Rules' (2009) 109(2) *Columbia Law Review* 396.

R.H. Coase, 'The Problem of Social Cost' (1960) 3 *Journal of Law and Economics* 1.

G.S. Geis, 'Empirically Assessing Hardley v. Baxendale' (2005) 33 *Florida State University of Law Review* 879.

G.S. Gies, 'An Experiment in the Optimal Precision of Contract Default Rules' (2006) 80 *Tulane Law Review* 1109.

C.P. Gillette, 'Standard Form Contracts', in G.D. Geest (Ed.), *Contract Law and Economics* (Cheltenham: Edward Elgar, 2011).

M. Kahan and M. Klausner, 'Standardization and Innovation in Corporate Contracting (or The Economics of Boilerplate)', (1997) 83 *Virginia Law Review*, 713.

A. Katz, 'The Economics of Form and Substance in Contract Interpretation' (2004) 104(2) *Columbia Law Review* 496.

R. Posner, 'The Law and Economics of Contract Interpretation' (2005) 83(6) *Texas Law Review* 1581.

Q. Zhou, 'An Economic Perspective on Legal Remedies for Unconscionable Contracts' (2010) 6(1) *European Review of Contract Law* 25.

Q. Zhou, 'What Can Contract Lawyers Learn from Law and Economics' (2011) 30(1) *University of Tasmania Law Review* 157.

7 The economic context of contract law: Part 2

- Economic theories of legal remedies
- Debates on efficient breach
- Liquidated damages and penalty clauses
- Impossibility and impracticability
- Behavioural approach to contract law

Introduction

In the last chapter, we examined a number of economic questions prior to the stage of contract performance. In this chapter, we will discuss the key economic issues related to both the performance of contract and the post-performance stage. We will first investigate the main economic functions of the legal remedy for breach of contract, and then move on to the debate over the theory of efficient breach, one of the most controversial economic theories of contract law; after that, we discuss the party-agreed remedy for breach of contract and the excuses for performance. Finally, we will briefly review one of the new developments in the law and economics, that is, the behavioural economics of contract law.

Economic theories of legal remedies

According to conventional legal wisdom, the remedy for the breach of a contract serves the purpose of corrective justice. In other words, when one party to a contract commits a wrong by breaching the contract, he inflicts harm on the other party. The legal remedy should correct this unjust outcome by forcing the breaching party to repair the unjust outcome by paying damages to the non-breaching party. The normal legal remedy for the breach of a contract is expectation damages, which will try to put the parties into the position in which they would have been had no breach been committed. After receiving compensation, the aggrieved party would be in the same position as he would had no contract been performed. The wrong is corrected and justice is restored.[1]

The economic theories of legal remedy for breach of contract focus more on the parties' incentives. There are two key questions here. First, how do the different legal remedies for breach of a contract modify the promisees' *ex ante* incentive to invest in the contract? Suppose that Jane, a restaurant owner, makes a contract with Tom, a builder, to refurbish her restaurant. Tom knows that some risks may prevent his completing the work on time, such as bad weather, the delay in delivery of materials and, perhaps, illness of his workers. He can reduce the risk of late competition by employing more workers or working overnight. But this increases Tom's cost. Jane expects a surge in business when the restaurant is re-opened. So, she would like to order some ingredients for her recipes in advance. But if Tom cannot complete the work on time, the food she buys will be wasted. How much should Jane invest in the contract? Her incentives vary in accordance with the legal remedy for breach of the contract. Second, how does the legal remedy change the promisor's incentive to breach of a contract? A contract can be seen as an exchange of promises for future performances. When the future differs from what the party expects at the time of making the contract, he faces the decision as to whether he should perform the contract or simply breach it. He may believe that the value of the performance that he will receive from the other party is no longer worth the performance he will provide, and therefore, decide to breach the contract. The legal remedy for breach of a contract will change his incentives. In short, the economic theory of the legal remedy addresses two key questions. First, how can the legal remedy for breach of contract induce the parties to make an optimal investment in the contract? Second, how can the legal remedy create an incentive for the parties to breach the contract when the performance is not efficient anymore. We will deal with the two questions in turn.

But first, let us have a very brief review of the different types of remedy for breach of contract. Two major remedies for breach of contract are damages and specific performance. Conventionally, the remedy of damages can be further classified into three categories, namely, expectation damages, reliance damages, and restitutionary damages.[2] As an illustration, let us recall our previous example where Jane contracts Tom to refurbish the restaurant. Let us assume that Jane's restaurant is worth £100,000 before the refurbishment. She pays £20,000 to Tom, which assumes that, if Tom performs the contract properly, his performance will add an additional value of £50,000 to the restaurant. But Tom's performance does not meet the quality agreed by the parties; it creates an additional value of only £10,000. In addition, because

---

1   E. Weinbrib, *Corrective Justice* (Oxford: Oxford University Press, 2011), ch.3.
2   For general discussion of different types of damages, see E. McKendrick, *Contract Law*, 10th edn (Basingstoke: Palgrave Macmillan, 2012), pp.332–338.

of the lower quality of the refurbishment, a nearby company cancels its booking for Christmas dinner. As a consequence, Jane suffers a loss of £10,000. Furthermore, Jane also bought food and hired some casual staff for Christmas dinner, which costs her £5,000.

If the remedy of specific performance were awarded, the court would order Tom to redo the refurbishment to meet the requirement agreed by the parties. However, if the remedy of damages were granted, the compensation that Jane receives would vary according to the different type of damage.

Expectation damages will put the parties in the position in which they would have been had the contract been performed according to its terms. If Tom performed properly, Jane would receive an added value of £50,000, and the company would not cancel the booking. But now she only receives an added value of £10,000 and also suffers a loss of £10,000 as a result of that cancellation. The remedy of expectation damages would award her £50,000 (£50,000 – £10,000 + £10,000 = £50,000). However, reliance damages will maintain the parties in the same position in which they would have been had the parties not entered into the contract. Jane gives £20,000 to Tom in advance, but receives only £10,000 added value. She suffers a loss of £10,000 (£20,000 – £10,000 = £10,000) and also a cost of £5,000 paid for the food and casual workers for the Christmas dinner. She would not have suffered both losses had she not entered into the contract with Tom. Therefore, the remedy of reliance damages will award her £15,000. In addition, the remedy of restitution damages would restore to the parties the benefit which the parties confer on one another. If the remedy of restitutionary damages is awarded, Tom should return the benefit he received from Jane, (i.e., £20,000), and Jane should return to Tom the benefit that she received, the added value of £10,000. Therefore, Jane will receive compensation of £10,000.

Now let us examine the question of how the different legal remedies affect the promisee's incentives to invest in the contract. The contract provides the promisee with a form of insurance against the risk that the promisor breaches the contract. In many cases, the promisee may increase the value of the promisor's future performance by making additional investment in the contract. From an economic perspective, the legal remedy should induce the promisee to make an efficient investment. In other words, the benefit from the investment should exceed the cost of the investment. We begin our analysis with our previous example. Suppose that after signing the contract with Tom, the company is willing to book a Christmas dinner at Jane's restaurant. Jane will earn a profit of £10,000 from this deal. But she needs to order some foods and hire extra staff in advance. Both outlays cost her £5,000. However, if Tom's performance cannot meet the quality agreed in the contract, the company will cancel the booking. Moreover, there are two possible scenarios. In the first case, the chance that Tom's performance is satisfactory is 90 per cent; and in the second case, there is only 40 per cent chance that Tom's performance is satisfactory. The question is whether Jane should sign the contract with the Tom's company and invest £5,000 in advance. Apparently,

---

KEY TERM

Present value

Also known as the present discounted value. It reflects the value at present of the amount of the money in the future.

---

it is efficient for Jane to invest in the first case because the present value of the profit is £9,000 (£10,000 × 90% = £9,000), which is higher than the investment, £5,000.

The investment will make her a net profit of £4,000 at the present value. For this same reason, it is inefficient for her to invest in the second case, because the profit at the present value of the return from the investment is £4,000 (£10,000 × 40% + £4,000), which is lower than the value of the investment. If Jane invests £5,000, she will suffer a net loss of £1,500 at the present value (£4,000 − £5,000 = −£1,000). In an ideal world, the legal remedy should induce Jane to make the efficient investment. She should invest in the first case and not invest in the second case. Unfortunately, not every legal remedy is able to induce her to make the efficient investment. Let us examine each of them in turn.

First, the remedy of specific performance may induce Jane to make the efficient investment. Where the remedy of specific performance is granted, the court will order Tom to redo the refurbishment to meet the quality agreed by the party. If Jane invests £5,000 and Tom breaches the contract, the remedy of specific performance per se will not compensate Jane's £5,000, the cost of her investment or the expected profit from the investment, £10,000. In other words, this remedy does not provide her with insurance against the risk of her investment. This creates an incentive for her to make rational decision by only investing £5,000 in the first case. In economic jargon, the remedy of specific performance induces the promisee to internalise all of the cost of his or her decision on the investment. As a consequence, it creates an incentive for the promisee to make the efficient investment.

Second, the remedy of expectation damages may lead Jane to make the inefficient investment. If Jane invests £5,000 and Tom breaches the contract, the remedy of expectation damages will put Jane into the position she would have been in had the contract been performed properly. Therefore, Jane is able to recover the profit loss of £10,000 from her investment as part of expectation damages. The remedy of expectation damages provides Jane with a full insurance against the risk of her investment. Regardless of whether she makes an efficient or inefficient investment, she is guaranteed a profit from the investment. If Tom performs the contract properly, the company will pay her a profit of £10,000. If Tom breaches the contract, Tom will pay her £10,000 as the compensation for breach of contract. Therefore, she has the incentive to invest £5,000 regardless of whether or not it is efficient. In economic jargon, the remedy of expectation damages fully externalises the promisee's investment cost to the promisor thereby creating an perverse incentive for the promisee to make inefficient investment.

Third, the remedy of reliance damages may also induce Jane to make the inefficient investment. But its adverse effect is weaker than the remedy of expectation damages. Under the remedy of reliance damages, if Jane invests £5,000 and Tom breaches the contract, the remedy will put Jane into the position she would have been in had no contract been made. Therefore, she is only able to recover her investment cost, £5,000, and cannot recover the profit from the investment, £10,000. It is possible that Jane will still invest £5,000 in the second case, because if Tom performs the contract, she will make a profit of £10,000 from the company. But, if Tom breaches the contract, she can still be compensated for the investment cost of £5,000. After receiving the compensation, she is no worse off than had she not invested. This creates an incentive for her to invest even if it is inefficient. Nonetheless, this analysis is based on the assumption that Jane does not consider the opportunity cost of her investment.

If Jane does not invest £5,000 in the Christmas dinner outlay, she may invest £5,000 in an alternative business opportunity. Assume that this alternative can bring her a net profit of £1,000 at the present value. Apparently, she will not invest £5,000 in the second case where she will suffer a loss of £1,000 at the present value, but she is still willing to invest in the first case where she can make a profit of £9,000 at the present value. Therefore, the efficiency of reliance damages is uncertain. It is by and large dependent on the promisee's opportunity cost of the investment.

Fourth, the remedy of restitutionary damages may also induce Jane to invest efficiently. Under this remedy, where Jane invests £5,000 and Tom breaches the contract, Jane can neither recover her investment cost of £5,000, nor can she recover the profit from the investment, £10,000. Therefore, the remedy of restitutionary damages leads the promisee to internalise the full cost of his

---

KEY TERM

Opportunity cost

The cost of a best alternative that must be forgone in order to pursue a certain action. It is calculated as the benefit the actor could have received by taking an alternative action.

or her decision on the investment. It creates an incentive for him to make only the efficient investment.

This discussion shows that not every legal remedy induces the promisee to make an efficient investment in the contract. Both the remedy of specific performance and the remedy of restitutionary damages can create the incentive for an efficient investment because they cause the promisee internalise all of the costs from his investment. However, the remedy of expectation damages and the remedy of reliance damages may lead the promise to invest inefficiently because the promisee can externalise the cost from his investment to the promisor. However, the adverse effect is much stronger under the remedy of expectation damages as the promisee can externalise the full cost of the investment to the promisor. Under the remedy of reliance damages, the promisee can only externalise a part of the cost to the promisor. The adverse effect is dependent on the promisee's opportunity cost for the investment.

Now let us turn to the analysis the second key economic question in relation to the legal remedies for breach of a contract. How does the legal remedy affect the promisor's decision on breaching the contract?[3] It was shown in the last chapter that a contract can be a Pareto improvement of resource allocation, which makes both parties to a contract better off. Nonetheless, this by no means is to suggest that the performance of a contract is always efficient. If, after the contract is signed, the promisor's performance cost increases unexpectedly so that the promisor's performance cost is higher than the promisee's expected profit from the contract, it is inefficient to perform the contract. Rather, the breach of the contract is efficient. Let us use our previous example as an illustration. In our previous example, Jane can realise an expected profit of £50,000 from the contract with Tom; if Tom's performance cost increases to £80,000 because of the unexpected increase in market price for materials; if Tom performs the contract, he will suffer a loss of £80,000, but Jane only benefits £50,000. The net payoff will be −£30,000 (£50,000 − £80,000 = −£30,000). It is efficient for Tom to *breach* the contract rather than performing the contract. From a purely economic perspective, the performance is only efficient if the promisor's performance cost is lower than the promisee's benefit from the performance; while if the performance cost exceeds the promisee's benefit from the performance, it is efficient for the promisor to breach the contract. This proposition is called the *theory of efficient breach* in the literature of law and economics. It should be noted here, however, that the argument of efficient breach is a highly controversial proposition and has been subject to extensive criticism. We will return to this debate on the efficient breach in the next section. Our present purpose is to examine whether the different efficient breach can create an incentive for the promisor to commit an efficient breach.

---

3 For a formal analysis of legal remedies, see S. Shavell, 'Damage Measures for Breach of Contract' (1980) 11(2) *Bell Journal of Economics* 466.

First, the remedy of specific performance may prevent an inefficient performance, but it increases the transaction cost for the parties.[4] If Tom breaches the contract when his performance cost increases to £80,000 and Jane claims for the remedy of specific performance, the court will order Tom to perform the contract even though the performance cost is higher than Jane's expected profit from the performance. Consequently, the remedy of specific performance forces Tom to undertake an inefficient performance. But we must not conclude harshly that the remedy of specific performance gives rise to inefficient performance. There is a possibility that Tom may bribe Jane not to sue him for breach of the contract. If Tom performs the contract, he will suffer a cost of £80,000, so he may be willing to pay Jane any amount lower £80,000 for her to relinquish the remedy of specific performance. Tom's performance is worth only £50,000 to Jane, so Jane could be willing to accept any amount higher than £50,000 for the right to sue Tom. There is a chance that the parties may settle the dispute. Tom will pay Jane any figure between £50,000 and £80,000. If the parties reach a private settlement, inefficient performance will not happen. Of course, to achieve the settlement, the parties inevitably incur transaction costs. But as long as the transaction cost is lower than the total benefit from settlement, it is reasonable to say that the parties may reach an agreement. Thus, under the remedy of specific performance, an inefficient breach can be prevented, but the parties' transaction costs are higher.

Second, the remedy of expectation damages can facilitate an efficient breach.[5] If Tom breaches the contract and Jane claims for the remedy of expectation damages, Tom needs to pay Jane compensation of £50,000. Clearly, Tom will save £30,000 from breaching the contract (£80,000 − £50,000 = £30,000). The result is efficient. Under the remedy of expectation damages, the promisor must pay the promisee's expected profit from the contract. The promisor has the incentive to breach the contract as long as his performance cost is higher than the promisee's expected value in his performance, which is the expectation damages the promisor pays for his breach. The remedy of expectation damages creates a right incentive for the promisor. The promisor will only commit a breach when the breach is efficient. Compared with the remedy of specific performance, transaction costs are also lower under the remedy of expectation damages. The promisor does not need to negotiate with the promisee when the performance turns out to be inefficient.

Third, both the remedy of reliance damages and the remedy of restitutionary damages may lead to an inefficient breach. If Tom breaches the contract and Jane claims for either reliance damages or restitutionary damages, Tom will

---

4 T. Ulen, 'The Efficiency of Specific Performance: Toward a Unified Theory of Contract Remedies' (1984) 83 *Michigan Law Review* 341.
5 R. Birmingham, 'Breach of Contract, Damage Measures, and Economic Efficiency' (1970) 24(2) *Rutgers Law Review* 273.

pay Jane a sum of compensation lower than the cost of performance. He will breach the contract anyway. So the outcome is efficient. However, the problem with both remedies is that the promisee's expectation interests are not fully protected and the promisee may have an incentive to breach the contract even though the breach is inefficient. Where the remedy of restitutionary damages is awarded, Tom will pay Jane a compensation of £10,000. Suppose now that Tom's performance cost is increased to only £20,000. If he breaches, he will suffer £10,000 as damages paid to Jane. If he performs, he will suffer a *loss of £20,000*. Clearly, then, he is going to breach the contract. But his breach is inefficient, because Jane's expected profit from the contract is £50,000. Tom's breach creates a social loss of £30,000 (£50,000 –£20,000 = £30,000). This example illustrates that both reliance damages and restitutionary damages create an incentive for the promisor to commit an inefficient breach.

In brief, the most efficient remedy is expectation damages that fully protect the promisee's expectation interests thereby creating an incentive for the promisor to breach the contract only if the breach is efficient. Furthermore, the remedy of specific performance can also prevent an inefficient performance. But it increases the parties' transaction costs, as the parties need to negotiate a private settlement when the performance becomes inefficient. Finally, both reliance damages and restitutionary damages are inefficient. Neither remedy protects the promisee's expectation interests thereby creating an incentive for the promisor to commit an inefficient breach.

The legal remedies for breach of a contract perform two economic functions. First, it should induce the promisee to make an efficient investment in the contract and, second, it should induce the promisor to beach the contract when the performance is inefficient. To achieve the first goal, the legal remedy must cause the promisee to internalise all of the costs from his investment. In other words, the legal remedy must not protect his full expectation interests. As once the promisee's expectation interests are fully protected, he will shift the risk of his decision to the promisor. Therefore, he will overinvest in the contract at a level greater than the optimal level. From this point of view the remedy of expectation damages is inefficient, and both reliance damages and restitutionary damages are efficient. However, to induce the promisor to commit an efficient breach, the legal remedy must protect the promisee's expectation interests. Otherwise, the promisor will not take a full account of the promisee's value in the performance when deciding whether or not to breach the contract. So, from this point of view, the remedy of expectation damages is efficient, and both reliance damages and restitutionary damages are inefficient. It is very hard to achieve both goals simultaneously. This problem is called the *paradox of compensation* in the literature of law and economics.[6] This seems to suggest that the remedy of specific performance is superior to the remedy of damages. It can induce the promisee to make an

6 R. Cooter, 'Unity in Tort, Contract and Property: The Model of Precaution' (1985) 73(1) *California Law Review* 1.

efficient investment in the contract as it does not fully protect the promisee's expected profit from the contract. At the same time, it also can induce the parties to reach a private settlement to prevent an inefficient performance. Table 7.1 summarises the economic features of the legal remedies discussed in this section.

Debates on efficient breach

Among all the economic theories of contract law, the theory of efficient breach is probably the most controversial proposition and it has been widely criticised on a number of grounds.[7] In this section, we explore some major criticisms of this theory. As discussed earlier, the simple version of the efficient breach suggests that the promisor should breach the contract when his performance cost exceeds the promisee's expected benefit from the performance. This type of breach satisfies the Kaldor-Hick standard of efficiency, which requires that the breach will, in aggregate, generate more gains than losses.[8]

Table 7.1 Types of legal remedy

	Specific performance	*Expectation damages*	*Reliance damages*	*Restitutionary damages*
Efficient investment	Yes	No	Possible (it depends on opportunity costs	Yes
Efficient breach	Yes (high transaction costs)	Yes	No (too many inefficient breaches)	No (too many inefficient breaches)

KEY TERM

Kaldor-Hicks efficiency

A measure of efficiency named after two famous economists, Nicholas Kaldor and John Hicks. A legal rule is Kaldor-Hicks efficient if it generates more gains than losses in total.

---

7 For general discussion, see I. Macnell, 'Efficient Breach of Contract: Circles in the Sky' (1982) 68(5) *Virginia Law Review* 947; D. Friedmann, 'The Efficient Breach Fallacy' (1989) 18(1) *Journal of Legal Studies* 1; S. Dawinder, 'A Crisis of Confidence and Legal Theory: Why the Economic Downturn Should Help Signal the End of the Doctrine of Efficient Breach' (2011) 24 *Georgetown Journal of Legal Ethics* 357.
8 A. Ogus, Costs and Cautionary Tales Economic Insights for the Law (Oxford: Hart Publishing, 2006), p.27.

This version of efficient breach does not take sufficient consideration of the promisee's interests. As long as the total gains outweigh the total losses, the breach is efficient even though the promisee's personal losses are not fully compensated. From a conventional lawyer's perspective, a breach of contract is a wrong, which generates an unjust outcome. The legal remedy for breach of a contract serves a purpose of corrective justice by compensating the full losses of the promisee. Apparently this version of efficient breach is in the conflict with the fundamental value of contract law proposed by conventional lawyers.[9] Furthermore, even from an economic perspective, this version of efficient breach is also problematic. According to this proposition, only the gain and loss resulting from the breach should be taken into account in aggregation, (i.e., the promisee's private losses do not matter). Therefore, it is not necessary to design the legal remedy to compensate the promisee's full losses, as long as the legal remedy encourages the breach that generates a total gain more than the total loss. However, as we discussed in the last chapter, the law of contract is supposed to provide the party with an insurance against the risk of breach of the contract by the other party. Once the latter party commits a breach, the legal remedy should put the former party into the position he would have been in had no breach been committed. If the legal remedy aimed to encourage the Kaldor-Hicks efficient breach rather than compensating the party's full losses, the parties would have less incentive to make the contract in the first place. The economic function of contract law is also undermined. For the reasons noted earlier, this version of efficient breach has become unpopular in the literature of law and economics.

A more popular version of efficient breach is developed from a proposition made by a renowned American judge, Oliver Wendell Holmes. In the analysis of contract law remedy in his seminal paper entitled 'The Path of the Law', he makes a famous remark: 'The duty to keep a contract at common law means a prediction that you must pay damages if you do not keep it – and nothing else'.[10]

The underlining idea is that the promisor has the option either to perform the contract or to breach the contract and to pay the promisee expectation damages, which should put the promisee into the position he would have been in had the promisor not breached the contract. According to this version of efficient breach, the breach makes nobody worse off. The promisor saves the performance cost, and the promisee, after receiving the compensation, is in the position no different from that had the contract been performed. Therefore, this version of efficient breach satisfies the requirement of Pareto improvement. The breach makes the promisor better off by saving him the performance cost but neither does it make the promisee worse off.[11]

---

9 R. Stevens, 'Damages and the Right to Performance: A Golden Victory or Not?', in J. Neyers, R. Bronaugh and S. Pitel (Eds.), *Exploring Contract Law* (Oxford: Hart Publishing, 2009), p.172.

10 O. W. Holmes, 'The Path of the Law' (1897) 10 *Harvard Law Review* 457, at 462.

11 For an overview of this version of efficient breach, see R. Craswell, 'Contract Remedies, Renegotiation, and the Theory of Efficient Breach' (1988) 61 *Southern California Law Review* 628.

Following this reasoning, many scholars of law and economics argue that the remedy of expectation damages is more efficient than the remedy of specific performance, because it allows the promisor to commit a Pareto-efficient breach. In other words, when the promisor finds that his performance cost exceeds the promisee's expectation interests in the contract, he can choose to breach the contract instead of performing. Conversely, the remedy of specific performance will force the promisor to perform the contract, even though the breach is efficient. Under the remedy of expectation damages, damages are perceived as a price that the promisor pays for his illegal behaviour, the breach of the contract. Therefore, the law of contract actually operates a system of implicit pricing by setting the price for the breach of a contract.[12]

In fact, the efficiency merit of expectation damages is exaggerated. First, the achievement of the efficient result does not necessarily need a breach of contract.[13] Where the promisor's performance cost increases to the level higher than the promisee's expected gain from the performance, the promisor will have an incentive to negotiate with the promisee to terminate the contract. A rational promisee would be willing to accept a sum higher than his expected gain to relinquish his right to the performance. The promisor would be willing to pay the promisee a sum lower than his performance cost. Where the transaction costs are negligible, the efficient outcome can be achieved through the private negotiation.[14] The promisor does not need to breach the contract, neither does the legal remedy matter. The only economic significance of the remedy of expectation damages is that it saves the transaction cost for the party. Instead of negotiating with the promisee, the promisor can simply breach the contract and pay damages to the promisee.

Second, should we then be able to say that the remedy of expectation damages is more efficient? Not necessarily. As an illustration, let us compare the remedy of expectation damages with the remedy of specific performance. Which remedy is the more efficient? The answer depends on which one generates the lower cost. Of course, under the remedy of specific performance, the transaction cost is higher. But under the remedy of expectation damages, the promisee will sue the promisor when the promisor commits the contract. Other things being equal, the litigation cost is higher under the remedy of expectation damages. To evaluate the efficiency characteristics of the two remedies, we need to compare the litigation cost under the remedy of expectation damages with the transaction cost under the remedy of specific performance.[15] This is an empirical question that the theoretical analysis cannot answer. But it is appropriate to say that we cannot reach the conclusion with confidence that the remedy of expectation damages is always efficient.[16]

---

12 A. Ogus, Costs and Cautionary Tales Economic Insights for the Law (Oxford: Hart Publishing, 2006), pp. 10–11.

13 J. Morgain, *Great Debates Contract Law* (London: Palgrave Macmillan, 2012), p.241.

14 R. Coase, 'The Problem of Social Cost' (1960) 3 *Journal of Law and Economics* 1.

15 A. Schwartz, 'The Case for Specific Performance' (1979) 89 *Yale Law Journal* 271.

16 I. Macnell, 'Efficient Breach of Contract: Circles in the Sky' (1982) 68(5) *Virginia Law Review* 947, at 954.

Third, the most controversial aspect of the theory of efficient breach is related to the precise concept of efficiency. To further investigate this question, we need to distinguish the case in which the promisor breaches the contract for the purpose of saving the performance costs and the case where the promisor breaches the contract for the purpose of making a higher profit. The breach to save the performance cost is illustrated by our previous example of the contract between Jane and Tom. When Tom's performance cost exceeds Jane's expectation gain from the contract, Tom commits a breach. It is efficient because of two reasons. First, as to Tom, the breach saves his private performance cost. Second, from a standpoint of society as a whole, it is also efficient. If Jane's expectation gains are less than Tom's performance costs, the performance generates a net loss. The resources and efforts invested in the performance are wasted. Tom's breach is not only efficient for Tom himself, but also efficient for society because it prevents the waste of resources.

Nonetheless, where the breach is committed to make a higher profit, it is highly controversial whether or not the breach is efficient for society.[17] Suppose Michael is willing to sell his car for £10,000, and Rob values Michael's car at a price of £15,000. So he purchases the car from Michael. Before Michael delivers the car to Rob, John offers him £20,000 to buy the car. Michael sells the car to John and pays Rob the compensation of £5,000, which will put the Rob in the position he would have been had Michael not breached the contract. The breach makes Michael better off by £5,000 than selling the car to Rob. It also makes John better off, because he must value the car as worth more than £20,000, otherwise he would not be buying it from Michael. Furthermore, the breach makes Rob no worse off as he receives a compensation of £5,000. His welfare is no different from the one if Michael performs the contract. This is a typical example of Pareto-efficient breach. The breach makes two parties better off and nobody worse off. We must ask the question as to whether the breach increases social wealth. Of course it does not. What the breach actually does is to redistribute the wealth among the parties. The breach allocates the property in the car to John and takes a sum of £20,000 from John, giving £15,000 to Michael and £5,000 to Rob. The aggregate of social welfare is unchanged. The only difference is that if Michael does not breach the contract, the car will belong to Rob and Michael will receive £10,000 from Rob. The breach only redistributes John's £20,000 to Michael and Rob. This certainly does not increase the social wealth. It is just a redistribution of the existing social wealth.

The supporters of the theory of efficiency breach will argue that the breach leads to allocative efficiency by allocating the car to its highest value user (i.e., John). But this can actually be achieved without breach. If Michael does not breach the contract, the car will be first sold to Rob. For him, the car is worth

17 For an overview, see R. Cotter, and T. Ulen, *Law and Economics*, 5th edn (London: Pearson, 2007), pp.266–269.

£15,000. John values the car at £20,000. Certainly, Rob would be happy to sell the car to John at a price higher than £15,000. Eventually, the car still moves to its highest valuer, John. There is no difference in the allocative efficiency between the case in which Michael breaches the contract with Rob and sells the car to John and the case in which Michael performs the contract with Rob and Rob sells the car to John. The breach allows Michael to benefit from the sale and the performance allows Rob to benefit. This is merely a redistribution of the wealth and the allocative efficiency is the same.[18]

The final major criticism of the theory of efficient breach is that it is not a Pareto improvement. It actually makes the promisee worse off.[19] If the comparison is made between the case in which the promisor breaches the contract and the case in which the promisor performs the contract, the promisee is not made worse off. In our example, Rob is compensated for his expectation loss of £5,000. However, if the comparison takes the resale to the third party into consideration, the promisee is made worse off. If the promisor breaches the contract, he can benefit from the resale to the third party. In contrast, if the promisor performs the contract, the promisee will benefit from the resale. The promisor's breach actually deprives the promisee of the benefit from the resale, and makes him worse off than the case in which the contract is performed. In our example, Michael's breach brings a gain of £5,000 to himself. However, if Michael performs the contract, Rob will benefit from selling the car to John. Michael's breach deprives Rob of the gain from the resale with John. Reasoning in this way, we cannot say that the breach is a Pareto improvement, as Rob is rendered worse off.

Liquidated damages and penalty clauses

In both common law jurisdictions and civilian law jurisdictions, the law of contract provides only the default remedy for the breach of contract, which is expectation damages in a common law jurisdiction and specific performance in a civilian jurisdiction. The parties can agree on their own legal remedy to replace the default ones. Frequently, in particular in many commercial contracts, the parties will agree a clause that stipulates the sum of damages for a breach of contract or a method to calculate damages. In civilian jurisdictions, the party-agreed remedy is subject to less legal restriction; whereas it is controlled tightly in common law jurisdictions.[20] The party-agreed damages can be further divided into two kinds, namely the liquidated damages

---

18 Q. Zhou, 'Is a Seller's Efficient Breach of Contract Possible in English Law?' (2008) 24(3) *Journal of Contract Law* 268, at 278.

19 J. Morgan, *Great Debate Contract Law* (London: Palgrave Macmillan, 2012), pp.240–243.

20 U. Mattei, 'The Comparative Law and Economics of Penalty Clauses' (1995) 43 *American Journal of Comparative Law* 427; A. Hatzis, 'Having the Cake and Eating it Too: Efficient Penalty Clauses in Common and Civil Contract Law' (2002) 22 *International Review of Law and Economics* 381.

clause and the penalty clause. The liquidated damages clause is defined as a genuine pre-estimate of the loss that is likely to be occasioned by the breach. The penalty clause is, by way of contrast, defined as a clause that aims to punish the party for a breach of the contract. Often the amount of money stipulated in a penalty clause is unreasonably high. In a common law jurisdiction, only the liquidated damages clause is enforceable and the penalty clause is void.[21] Our present purpose is not to discuss the legal rule, but to examine the relevant economic questions in relation to a party-agreed remedy. One of the key economic questions is whether the legal prohibition in common law jurisdictions on penalty clauses is an economically good legal principle. There are still disagreements on the answer to this question.[22]

The economic explanation for writing a party-agreed remedy clause is that it is one solution to the problem of information asymmetry.[23] First, there is an information asymmetry between the judge and the parties. Writing a damage clause is costly. If the judge had perfect information as to the promisee's expectation losses generated by the promisor's breach, the promisee would be compensated perfectly for his expectation losses. There would be no need for a party-agreed damages clause. However, the judge normally does not have as same an amount of information as the parties do, and often it is very hard to verify the information as to the promisee' expectation losses. In particular, when the promisee attaches an idiosyncratic value to the contract. Consequently, the judge may make errors in the calculation of the promisee's expectation losses; then the judicial error may lead to economic problems. Where damages awarded by judges systematically undercompensates the promisee, it may lead the promisor to commit more inefficient breaches and encourage the promisee to underinvest in the contract. Conversely, if damages systematically overcompensate the promisee, it discourages the promisor to commit efficient breach of the contract and leads the promisee to overinvest in the contract. It is reasonable to assume that the parties have better information than the judge. The party-agreed damages clause can overcome the problems of both undercompensation and overcompensation. The legal prohibition on the penalty clause invites the judge to determine the validity of the party-agreed damages clause and it increases the risk of judicial error. Therefore, it is undesirable from an economic perspective. On the basis of this analysis, many law and economic scholars argue that the legal rule on the

---

21   For a overview of legal rules, see E. McKendrick, *Contract Law*, 10th edn (London: Palgrave Macmillan, 2013), pp.362–372.

22   S. Walt, 'Penalty Clauses and Liquidated Damages', in G.D. Geest (Ed.), *Contract Law and Economics* (Cheltenham: Edward Elgar, 2011), pp.178–179.

23   C.J. Geotz, and R.E. Scott, 'Liquidated Damages, Penalties and the Just Compensation Principle: Some Notes on an Enforcement Mode and a Theory of Efficient Breach' (1977) 77 *Colombia Law Review* 554.

party-agreed remedy in civilian law jurisdictions is more efficient than its counterpart in common law jurisdictions.[24]

Second, there is also an information asymmetry between the promisor and the promisee. In many contracts, the parties make a commitment to the performance in the future. But how creditable is the promise made the promisor? This piece of information is unverifiable not only to the judge, but also to the promisee. Given the fact that the default legal remedy may undercompensate the promisee for his expectation losses, the promisee may have less incentive to enter into the contract with the promisor in the first place. To increase his creditability, the promisor may agree on a penalty clause under which he will pay a very high damages to the promisee if he breaches the contract. The purpose of the penalty clause is like a 'signal' that shows that he is very confident in his performance thereby to increasing the credibility of his promise. In addition, the penalty clause also serves a function of insurance for the promise to against the risk of the promisor's breach. Some law and economics scholars argue that the legal prohibition on penalty clauses undermine this economic function, discouraging the parties to reach private solutions to the problem of information asymmetry.

It should also be noted that the penalty clause may give rise to a number of undesirable problems. First, it may encourage the promisees opportunistic behaviour. Because the amount of damages are very high, the promisee may have incentive to sue the promisor for breach of the contract even though he does not have a reasonable ground. Because the stakes are so high, he may gamble on the judicial error that leads the judge to award penalty damages to him.

Second, it may further exacerbate the information problem in the market.[25] Suppose that there are two types of construction company in the market, namely the good company and the bad company. The good company can always provide high-quality services, and the bad company only provides high-quality service occasionally. Because the quality of their work can only be shown after the building work is completed. It is very hard to judge which company is the good one at the time of making the contract. Therefore, the good company will have an incentive to distinguish itself from the bad company. One strategy is to insert a penalty clause in the contract to show his confidence in the quality of its work. To recoup the cost of the penalty clause, the good company may charge a higher contract price. But the bad company is willing to make more profit. It may pretend to be a good company by including the same penalty clause in the contract and also charging a higher price. Consumers still cannot distinguish the good company from the bad

24 A. Schwartz, 'The Myth that Promisees Prefer Supercompensatory Remedies: An Analysis of Contracting for Damages Measures' (1990) 100 *Yale Law Journal* 369.

25 P. Aghion, and B. Hermalin, 'Legal Restrictions on Private Contracts can Enhance Efficiency' (1990) 6 *Journal of Law, Economics* 381–409.

company. But there is a problem. The contract price in the construction market is increased because every contract has a penalty clause. Some consumers may be willing to pay a higher price for the penalty clause, but others may not. In fact, the latter are forced to purchase the penalty clause that they do not want. The legal prohibition on penalty clauses can solve this problem. It forbids the good company including the penalty clause in its contract. It does not need to charge a high price to cover the cost of the penalty clause. Accordingly, the bad company is not able to charge a high price by pretending to be the good company. The problem is solved.

Third, the parties are vulnerable to cognitive errors that may induce him to agree on a penalty clause to which he would not agree if he was behaving rationally. Studies in behavioural law and economics show that people are often irrationally optimistic.[26] They think that good things are more likely to happen than bad things. This bias may make the promisor overconfident in his performance. His decision to agree a penalty clause may be irrational. In addition, people often do not calculate the probability of a future event in a scientific way. They tend to do it by intuition and imagination, which can also lead to a wrong decision on the penalty clause.[27] The legal prohibition on penalty clauses can solve this problem by eliminating the chance for the party to agree to an irrational penalty clause.

Finally, the penalty clause may also have an anti-competitive effect on the market.[28] Suppose that all of the consumers sign their mobile phone contract with the only provider in the market, Company O. It writes a penalty clause into its contracts requiring its customers to pay a penalty if they terminate their contract. Now there are a number of firms intending to enter into the market. In order to attract consumers, they must offer both high-quality services and an attractive price. However, to compete with Compete O, the new companies must provide a very low price to justify Company O's customers' terminating their existing contract. In other words, the new firms actually pay the penalty for Company O's customers to terminate their existing contracts. Apparently, it increases significantly the service cost of the new firms, making them less competitive. This reasoning applies to all commercial sectors. The existing firm will have an incentive to include a penalty clause in their customers' contracts in order to increase their new competitor's cost. As a consequence, consumers are worse off due to the imperfect competition in the market. They pay a higher price, but they receive a lower quality service. This is another justification for the legal prohibition on penalty clauses. It prevents existing firms from using

26 D. Kahneman, and A. Tversky, 'On the Reality of Cognitive Illusions' (1996) 103 *Psychological Bulletin* 582.

27 M. Eisenberg, 'The Limits of Cognition and the Limits of Contracts' (1995) 47 *Stanford Law Review* 211.

28 P. Aghion, and P. Bolton, 'Contracts as Barriers to Entry' (1987) 77 *American Economic Review* 388.

penalty clauses to maintain their dominant position in the market. The cost of entry to the market is reduced. It encourages new firms to compete with the existing firms. Consumers can eventually benefit from their competition.

The economic analysis of the penalty clause shows that the party-agreed damages clause is a double-edged sword. On the one hand, it can be used to solve the problem of information asymmetry between the parties and judges or the parties themselves; on the other hand, it also generates a number of new problems. It is very hard to answer the question if the legal prohibition on penalty clause is economically desirable. We must not come to the harsh conclusion that the legal rule in civilian law jurisdictions is more efficient than its counterpart in common law jurisdictions simply because a penalty clause is enforceable in the former. The economic analysis of penalty clauses cannot provide a definite answer to the question as to whether or not the penalty clause should be enforced.

Impossibility and impracticability

Should the law of contract excuse the party's performance if his performance is physically impossible or the cost of his performance increases considerably so that the performance is impractical? In English law, this problem is addressed by the doctrine of *frustration*. Under this doctrine, a contract may be discharged if after the contract is made an unforeseeable event makes the performance of the contract physically impossible.[29] In *Taylor v Caldwell*,[30] the defendant let out the Surrey Gardens and Music Hall as the venue for the plaintiffs' concerts. Before the first concert, the hall was destroyed by fire. It was held that the defendant was not liable for breach of contract, because an unforeseeable event made the performance impossible. However, the doctrine of frustration in English contract law does not excuse the parties' performance merely because the performance becomes impracticable. In *Davis Contractors Ltd v Fareham Urban DC*,[31] the appellants agreed to build some houses for the respondents in eight months for £94,000. Because of labour shortages, the work took 22 months and cost the appellants £115,000. They argued that the contract had been frustrated and that the respondents should pay the extra remuneration. The House of Lord rejected this claim. Lord Radcliffe said:

> It is not hardship or inconvenience or material loss itself which calls the principal of frustration into play. There must be as well such a change in the significance of the obligation that the thing undertaken would, if performed, be a different thing from the contracted for.[32]

29 E. Peel, *Treitel on the Law of Contract*, 13th edn, (Sweet & Maxwell: London, 2010), p.920.
30 (1863) 3 B & S 826.
31 [1956] AC 696.
32 *Ibid*. at 729.

In contrast, the impracticability may discharge the contract in the US contract law. The impracticality includes reasons such as extreme and unreasonable difficulty, expense, and injury or loss to one of the parties. Examples include a severe shortage of raw materials of supplies due to war, embargo, local crop failure, or unforeseen shutdown of major sources of supplies that significantly increase the cost of performance.[33]

There are two economic questions in relation to the doctrine of frustration: first, does it perform any economic function? and, second, should the contract be discharged if the performance is still possible but becomes impractical or not?

It is suggested in the literature of contract law and economics that the doctrine of frustration can be used to induce the parties to achieve the efficient allocation of the risk.[34] It is reasonable to assume that the parties have the information advantage as to the variety of risks related to the performance contract. It is efficient for them to allocate the risks in the contract among themselves rather than asking judges to do it. Efficiency requires the risk to be allocated to the party who can manage the risk at the lower cost. Such a party is called the superior risk bearer. The doctrine of frustration can induce the parties to allocate the risk to the superior risk bearer. Where the doctrine is in operation, the promisor would be excused for his performance. Even though he is unable to perform his contractual obligations, he is not liable to the promisee for breach of the contract. Literally, the doctrine of frustration allocates the loss resulting from the promisor's non-performance to the promisee. In other words, the doctrine allocates the risk causing the promisor's non-performance to the promisee. On the contrary, if the doctrine of frustration does not apply, the promisor will be liable for his breach and pay damages to the promisee. The risk causing the non-performance is allocated to the promisor. Efficiency requires assigning the risk to the superior risk bearer. Accordingly, two implications can be drawn from this analysis.

First, the doctrine of frustration should be in operation to excuse the promisor's performance, if the promisee is the superior risk bearer. Second, the doctrine of frustration should not apply and the promisor should be held liable for breach of contract if he is the superior risk bearer. By doing so, the cost from the materialisation of the risk is allocated to the superior risk bearer. This legal rule creates an incentive for him to manage the risk, such as buying insurance against the risk.

The same line of reasoning is also applicable to the doctrine of mitigation in the law of contract. The doctrine of mitigation requires the promisee to mitigate his losses resulting from the promisor' breach of the contract. The promisee is unable to claim the amount of losses that would have been

---

33 E. Peel, *Treitel on the Law of Contract*, 13th edn (Sweet & Maxwell: London, 2010), p.937.
34 R. Posner, and A. Rosenfield, 'Impossibility and Related Doctrines in Contract Law: An Economic Analysis' (1977) 6 *Journal of Legal Studies* 221.

prevented had the promisee taken the reasonable step to mitigate. Where the promisor breaches the contract, the promisee is the best person to evaluate the losses generated by the promisor and to find the appropriate ways to reduce the losses. For example, in a sale contract of generic goods, if the seller breaches the contract, the buyer can buy the goods from an alternative seller. If it is the buyer who breaches the contract, the seller can reduce his losses by selling the goods immediately to another buyer. The duty of mitigation allocates the losses to the party who is best able to minimise it. Therefore, it creates an incentive for them to do so.[35]

Now let us turn to the second question. Should a contract be discharged if the promisor's performance is still possible, but it becomes impracticable (e.g., as the cost of the performance is increased rapidly). Some scholars of law and economics suggest that the doctrine of implacability should be applied in the same way as the doctrine of frustration. Both of them can induce the superior risk bearer to manage the risk.[36] In a seminal paper, Joskow provides an economic analysis of the doctrine of impracticability in a famous US instance, the *Westinghouse case*.[37] Westinghouse had contracted with several utilities to provide uranium fuel for their nuclear power plants at a fixed price. The cost of the uranium materials used to produce the uranium fuel increased more than Westinghouse had anticipated. The increase in the market price caused the failure of the industry to invest its long-term supply capacity to demand. Westinghouse was a major player in the industry and contributed largely to this result. The economic question is whether or not Westinghouse can discharge its contracts on the ground of impracticability. Joskow argues that the doctrine of impracticability should not be in operation in this case so that it allocates the loss resulting from the increase of the market price to Westinghouse, which was the superior risk bearer in comparison with its contractors. It can manage the risk by making proper investment in the long-term supply of the materials. It would be induced to manage the risk by placing the loss on it. In line with this analysis, it is suggested that the doctrine of impracticability should be applied if the following conditions are met: (1) the underlying condition of the contract must fail; (2) the failure must have been unforeseen at the time of contracting; (3) the risk of the failure must not have been assumed by the party seeking secure; (4) the performance must have been made impracticable; and (5) the party seeking the excuse must have made all reasonable attempts to ensure that his performance would be delivered.[38]

35 C. Bruce, 'An Economic Analysis of the Impossibility Doctrine' (1982) 11 *Journal of Legal Studies* 311.

36 D. Smythe, 'Impossibility and Impracticability', in G.D. Geest (Ed.), *Contract Law and Economics* (Edward Elgar: Cheltenham, 2011), p.210.

37 P. Joskow, 'Commercial Impossibility: The Uranium Market and the Unanticipated Price Changes' (1977) 6 *Journal of Legal Studies* 119.

38 D. Smythe, 'Impossibility and Impracticability', in G.D. Geest (Ed.), *Contract Law and Economics* (Edward Elgar: Cheltenham, 2011), p.211.

Behavioural approach to contract law

The modern law and economics movement started at the University of Chicago in the early 1960s. A small number of economists and lawyers applied economic methodologies to the study of law; then this approach was rapidly adopted by academics in the United States in a wide range of legal subjects. Later, it gradually spread to Europe and the rest of the world. Contract law is one of the most successful legal fields to which economic analysis applied. However, after five decades, the output produced by economic analysis make but a small contribution to the reform of contract law even in the United States, widely regarded as the birthplace of law and economics. Neither do judges and lawmakers adopt an economic approach in their judicial decisions and legislation, nor does economic theory explain satisfactorily most of the doctrines in contract law.[39]

One of the major criticisms is related to the assumption of rational choice on which the economic analysis of contract law is based. It is assumed that every individual is the best person to make decisions for himself and never makes mistakes. Clearly, this is untrue. People are vulnerable to a number of psychosocial biases. An emerging subfield of law and economics, called behavioural law and economics, has provided many new insights in understanding contractual behaviour.[40]

One of the key insights provided by the study of behavioural law and economics in contract law is related to default rules and standard form contracts. The studies in behavioural law and economics show that the default setting has a feature of stickiness because of people's status quo bias. Therefore, the sophisticated party may exploit the bias of the less sophisticated party, such as in consumer contracts. Research in psychology finds that people have an exaggerated preference for the present state of the world to any alternative states. Other things being equal, they prefer to leave things as they are rather than try something new.[41] In a contract, the status quo bias reflects the fact that the parties do not like to contract out the default terms in the contract. Once they sign the contract, they prefer the default terms and are very reluctant to make any effort to change them.[42] This creates an opportunity for traders to exploit consumers. For example, the trader can draft the contracts such that the consumers are obligated to make monthly payment but can stop making payments and return the goods at any time. Once the first monthly

---

39 E. Posner, 'Economic Analysis of Contract Law after Three Decades; Success or Failure?' (2003) 112 *Yale Law Journal* 829,

40 A. Vandenberghe, 'Behavioral Approach to Contract Law', in G.D. Geest (Ed.), *Contract Law and Economics* (Edward Elgar: Cheltenham, 2011), p.401.

41 D. Kahneman, J. Knetsch and R. Thaler, 'Experimental Tests of the Endowment Effect and the Coase Theorem' (1990) 98 *Journal of Political Economy* 1325.

42 R. Korobkin, 'Inertia and Preference in Contract Negotiation: The Psychological Power of Default Rules and Form Terms' (1998) 51 *Vanderbilt Law Review* 1583.

payment is made, the consumers, due to status quo bias, are very unlike to discontinue the contract and return the goods.[43] Therefore, the regulation of standard form contracts should be introduced to prevent traders exploiting consumers.

In addition, people are bounded rational beings and make persistent mistakes even though they have perfect information as to their decision making.[44] As a consequence, contracting parties, in particular consumers, often miscalculate the benefits and costs associated with the product and purchase products they would not have done had they been rational. They frequently express regret as to their purchases. This provides a very invaluable implication for the reform of consumer contract law. According to these findings, it is not enough to improve consumer protection by just addressing the problem of information deficiency. Even though the law provides an environment in which consumers can make informed decisions, they can still make the wrong choice. More legal rules should be introduced to address the bounded rationality of consumers. One such example would be a 'cooling-off' period. The law allows consumers to return the goods for a short period of time after the purchase without giving a reason to the trader. This provides consumers with an opportunity to think more carefully about whether they really want/need the goods.[45]

These illustrations are just two of many valuable insights provided by behavioural law and economics.[46] The value of traditional law and economics is undermined by the assumption of rational choice. Behavioural law and economics offers more accurate models of human behaviour based on solid empirical research. The findings can then help policymakers to improve the existing legal rules. One of the most successful areas currently being conquered by behavioural law and economics is consumer contract law. The behavioural approach broadens our understanding of consumers' behaviour. The findings reveal a number of psychological biases, which make consumers vulnerable to exploitation. These research outputs can help policymakers to reform consumer law and to improve protection for consumers. Certainly, the contributions of behavioural law and economics are not limited to the area of consumer law. It has also make valuable contributions to employment contract law and the regulation of long-term and other financial contracts.[47]

---

43 A. Vandenberghe, 'Behavioral Approach to Contract Law', in G.D. Geest (Ed.), *Contract Law and Economics* (Edward Elgar: Cheltenham, 2011), p.419.

44 M. Faure and H. Luth, 'Behevioural Economics in Unfair Contract Terms: Cautions and Considerations' (2011) *Journal of Consumer Policy* 337.

45 O. Bar-Gill, 'Bundling and Consumer Misperception' (2006) 98 *Northwestern University Law Review* 1373.

46 For more overview, see C. Sustein, 'Behavioral Analysis of Law' (1997) 64 *University of Chicago Law Review* 1175; R. Thaler and C. Sustein, *Nudge: Improving Decisions About Health, Wealth and Happiness* (London: Penguin, 2009).

47 C. Sunstein, *Simpler the Future of Government* (London: Simon & Schuster, 2013).

Behavioural law and economics certainly provides a new direction for the economic analysis of contract.

Key figures in law and economics

There are some major academic figures you will come across as you read more about law and economics – some of whom have already been referenced here (if you are checking the footnotes!), so this short section consists of a small amount of background to the major 'stars' in this area in the form of brief biographical notes.

BIO NOTE

Ronald Harry Coase was born in 1910 in Willesden, London, and was educated at Kilburn Grammar School and the London School of Economics (LSE). After graduating with the degree of Bachelor of Commerce he became Assistant Lecturer at the University of Liverpool before returning in 1935 to the LSE where he remained until 1951. In 1937 he married Marion Ruth Hartung, from Chicago. Following work at the University of Buffalo and the University of Virginia, Coase joined the University of Chicago in 1964. Seen as the principal founding father of law and economics, he was Clifton R. Musser Professor of Economics at Chicago and won the Nobel Prize in Economics in 1991 for his contribution to the field of institutional economics. He is the author of two seminal papers entitled, 'The Problem of Social Cost' and 'The Nature of Firm'.

Coase died in 2013 at the age of 102, surviving his wife by less than a year.

BIO NOTE

Richard Allen Posner was born in New York in 1939. He was educated at Yale where he majored in English and graduated in 1959 *summa cum laude*. From Yale he proceeded to Harvard Law School, graduating LLB *magna cum laude* and first in his class in 1962. He had also been president of the *Harvard Law Review*. He clerked for Justice Brennan in the US Supreme Court before becoming Attorney-Advisor to the Federal Trade Commissioner and subsequently worked in the Solicitor-General's office. In 1968 he took a teaching post at Stanford University before moving the following year to the University of Chicago Law School where he remains a Senior Lecturer, although in 1981, he was appointed by President Reagan as a judge of the US Court of Appeals, Seventh Circuit (in Chicago), a court on which he sat as Chief Judge from 1993 to 2000. He is married to Charlene and their son Eric is a professor at Chicago Law School.

He is seen as one of the founding fathers of law and economics.

BIO NOTE

George Arthur Akerlof was born in New Haven, Connecticut, in 1940 and educated at Lawrenceville School, Yale (BA, 1962) and Massachusetts Institute of Technology (PhD, 1966). He then joined the faculty at University of California, Berkeley, where he secured tenure in 1969. He spent time at the Indian Statistical Institute in 1967 and 1968 and as senior economist at the Council of Economic Advisors in 1973 and 1974. From 1978 to 1980 he taught at the London School of Economics having resigned from Berkeley. However, Berkeley had never accepted his resignation and he returned there in 1980 and is now Koshland Professor of Economics. He shared the 2001 Nobel Prize in Economics with Michael Spence and Joseph E. Stiglitz for their contribution to the study of problem of information asymmetry. His seminal paper entitled 'The Market for Lemons: Quality Uncertainty and Market Mechanism' is considered one of most important pieces in the literature of law and economics.

He is married to the distinguished economist Janet Yellan, a former member of the Federal Reserve Board. Their son, Robert, teaches economics at the University of Warwick.

BIO NOTE

Robert D. Cooter was born in 1945 and took his first degree, in psychology, at Swarthmore College (a liberal arts college near Phila-delphia in Pennsylvania) graduating in 1967. He went straight to Oxford University on a Fulbright Scholarship to study for a further BA, this time gaining first class honours in philosophy, politics and economics. From Oxford he went to Harvard where he obtained a PhD in economics in 1975. The same year he began a teaching job at the University of California, Berkeley, in the Department of Economics. He moved to the

School of Law in 1980, where he is Herman F. Selvin Professor of Law. Together with Thomas Ulen he is author of a popular textbook on law and economics: *Introduction to Law and Economics.*

He is married to Blair and they have three grown-up children.

BIO NOTE

Cass Robert Sunstein was born in Concord, Massachusetts, in 1954 and was educated locally at Middlesex School before studying at Harvard College (BA, 1975) and then Harvard Law School, from which he graduated with a JD, *magna cum laude*, in 1978. He served as clerk first to Justice Kaplan of the Massachusetts Supreme Court and then to Justice Thurgood Marshall of the US Supreme Court. Thurgood Marshall had been US Solicitor-General when Posner worked in the Solicitor-General's office. After a year working as an Attorney-Advisor in the Office of the Legal Counsel in the US Justice Department, he became Assistant Professor at the University of Chicago Law School, becoming full professor in 1985. In 1988 he was appointed Karl N. Llewellyn Professor in both law and political science, becoming Karl N. Llewellyn Distinguished Service Professor in 1993. In 2008 he moved to Harvard Law School where he is currently the Robert Walmsley University Professor and the Felix Frankfurter Professor of Law. From 2009 to 2012 he served the Obama administration as Administrator of the Office of Information and regulatory affairs.

He is married to his second wife, Samantha, and they have two children.

Suggested further reading

I.R. Macneil, 'Efficient Breach of Contract: Circles in the Sky' (1982) 68 *Virginia Law Review* 947.

P.G. Mahoney, 'Contract Remedies: General', in G.D. Geest (Ed.), *Contract Law and Economics* (Edward Elgar: Cheltenham, 2011).

A. Vandenberghe, 'Behavioral Approach to Contract Law', in G.D. Geest (Ed.), *Contract Law and Economics* (Edward Elgar: Cheltenham, 2011).

Index